THE
CHRISTMAS
EXPERIMENT

To my loving husband, Jay, and our four wonderful children, Daniel, Adam, Sheena, and Carianne, who have been so supportive of my efforts to have more meaningful Christmas celebrations.

Thanks also to my mother, Barbara, and my dear friend Debra, for their unwavering love and support, and to my kind editor, Kimiko Hammari, for her patience in helping me realize this dream.

THE CHRISTMAS EXPERIMENT

6 WAYS TO INCLUDE CHRIST IN YOUR FAMILY CHRISTMAS

DENISE WAMSLEY

Horizon Publishers • Springville, Utah

© 2010 Denise Wamsley

All rights reserved.

No part of this book may be reproduced in any form whatsoever, whether by graphic, visual, electronic, film, microfilm, tape recording, or any other means, without prior written permission of the publisher, except in the case of brief passages embodied in critical reviews and articles.

This is not an official publication of The Church of Jesus Christ of Latter-day Saints. The opinions and views expressed herein belong solely to the author and do not necessarily represent the opinions or views of Cedar Fort, Inc. Permission for the use of sources, graphics, and photos is also solely the responsibility of the author.

ISBN 13: 978-0-88290-975-2

Published by Horizon Publishers, an imprint of Cedar Fort, Inc., 2373 W. 700 S., Springville, UT 84663
Distributed by Cedar Fort, Inc., www.cedarfort.com

LIBRARY OF CONGRESS CATALOGING-IN-PUBLICATION DATA

Library of Congress Cataloging-in-Publication Data

Wamsley, Denise.
 Christmas experiment / Denise Wamsley.
  p. cm.
 ISBN 978-0-88290-975-2 (acid-free paper)
 1. Families--Religious life. 2. Christmas. 3. Christian life--Mormon authors. I. Title.

BX8643.F3W36 2010
263'.915--dc22

2010018049

Cover design by Angela D. Olsen
Cover design © 2010 by Lyle Mortimer
Edited and typeset by Kimiko Christensen Hammari

Printed in the United States of America

10 9 8 7 6 5 4 3 2 1

Printed on acid-free paper

TABLE OF CONTENTS

Preface vii

PART I: JOURNEY TO BETHLEHEM

Chapter 1: Following Yonder Star 3
Chapter 2: Bearing Gifts, We Traverse Afar 7
Chapter 3: We Three Kings 19
Chapter 4: Field and Fountain, Moor and Mountain 27

PART II: 6 STEPS TO A MORE MEANINGFUL CHRISTMAS

Chapter 5: Star with Royal Beauty Bright 37
Chapter 6: Simplify Gift Giving 51
Chapter 7: Give All Year 77
Chapter 8: Create Meaningful Family Experiences 85
Chapter 9: Serve One Another 109
Chapter 10: Teach with Symbolism 133
Chapter 11: Enjoy Quality Traditions 149
Chapter 12: Guide Us to Thy Perfect Light 161

PREFACE

Life is full of journeys. From the moment we are born until the day we die, we all embark on a forward path, our destiny defined by the choices we make and the directions we choose to travel.

This is not your average Christmas book. It is about a very personal journey I began many years ago to discover the true meaning of Christmas. I had become increasingly unhappy about how we celebrated the birth of our Savior and thus embarked on my spiritual journey to Bethlehem.

This trek to a more meaningful Christmas helped me formulate six distinct steps to bring Christ back into Christmas in a way that would help my family have sacred experiences and still enjoy the many meaningful activities that bind us together in love and unity. In essence, I developed a battle plan to overcome the materialism, consumerism, and busyness that had crept into our sacred holiday.

As we began to make changes in our family, a friend asked me to share my experiences with her Relief Society. Hungry for solutions to use in their own families, more people asked me to share my thoughts. What began as a personal journey to the manger blossomed into the opportunity to teach numerous workshops every year during the Christmas season for the next fifteen years.

I love to share my testimony and my feelings about this subject that is so close to my heart. Sharing my beliefs strengthens me and prepares me personally for a more meaningful season. I have been truly blessed by these choice opportunities. They have helped me fulfill a personal decision to give the gift of myself to my Savior at Christmas.

What I share with you here comes not from any sense of pride, or to boast of any success, because I know from whom my blessings flow. I desire only to bear testimony of the Savior and what He can do with our lives if we but come to Him with open hearts and willing hands. He will keep His promises, and we will be strengthened.

I am always astounded when people are interested in what I have to say. People often approach me at the store or another public place and say something like, "You're that Christmas lady, aren't you?" I'm grateful they remember me, and I take it as a compliment. But when they say their Christmases have changed because of me, I am always humbled and deeply touched.

In my Christmas workshops, I have shared the philosophies and practices that have helped me so much in my own journey. In addition, I asked those present to write down their most cherished Christmas traditions, and we took time to share some of these ideas. Over the years, this has provided me with many ideas that I share within these pages, along with many that I have gathered over the years from other sources and many that I have personally tried.

I have given many Internet sites as sources, and it is with the understanding that the information is subject to change. Websites shut down, change names, and so on. If you cannot find the correct site, please perform a search on the Internet to find current information.

I apologize in advance if my stories and examples seem too personal or detailed. Perhaps some readers will find my honesty uncomfortable, but this is a personal story about a personal struggle, and I cannot tell the whole story without becoming personal. I must share what I feel in my heart. These stories and examples have always been well received in my workshops because they serve as practical examples of the principles I try to teach. They are about my life and my choices, and the reader must use the Spirit to adapt these ideas to benefit his or her own family situation.

Ultimately, I hope that all who read this find something in these pages that will enlighten them, uplift them, and give them courage so that as disciples of Christ together we may move away from the world in the way we celebrate His birth and His life.

And now, enjoy the journey.

PART I

Journey to Bethlehem

We three kings of Orient are,
Bearing gifts we traverse afar,
Field and fountain, moor and mountain,
Following yonder star.

CHAPTER 1

Following yonder star

For years, I made great efforts to follow the light of the heavenly star I believed would lead me to Bethlehem. For as long as I can remember, my heart has yearned to have meaningful Christmas celebrations that encompass the love of family, friends, and neighbors. I struggled to create a beautiful and inviting home environment that would embrace the joyfulness of the season while giving my family the peace and serenity of knowing that God gave us His son and the reassurance that our activities and traditions were centered on the Savior.

Christmas is about joy and sharing and basking in the glow of love and friendship. It is heart-felt emotions that stir deep within us to prompt us to reach out to those whose needs are greater than our own. It's about making each moment count. Christmas is something you feel—"a voice, a chime, a chant sublime, of peace on earth, goodwill to men." It is the season of seasons, the most wonderful time of the year.

If this was the most wonderful time of the year, then why did I feel the way I did? Year after year, I felt unsuccessful in creating those meaningful Christmas celebrations. With each and every effort at creating the perfect Christmas, the star I was following seemed to fade further and further into the horizon.

Through the years, I tried many different ways to infuse true Christmas spirit into our seasons, but I just couldn't seem to accomplish what I wanted. Part of the problem was that I wasn't sure what I really wanted from Christmas, so I tried on a lot of different solutions like someone might try on pairs of shoes. But nothing ever fit!

In one of my early attempts, I tried to make my growing family's Christmas more special by following some well-intentioned advice. The way to make our season more meaningful, I was told, was to have a "homemade Christmas." This was the best way to give gifts because with every gift given, we would give a portion of ourselves. With enthusiasm, I knitted hats and scarves, made stuffed animals and toys, and even crafted an ottoman from wood and leather. I baked all kinds of wonderful goodies and handcrafted all the decorations for our tree. By the time Christmas Day arrived, I was exhausted. I had been very creative and conservative and had spent so much time and effort at making the season meaningful. So why was I left with a nagging sense of disappointment on Christmas morning? Hadn't I worked hard to make my homemade Christmas perfect?

The next year brought a new opportunity for me to make the homemade Christmas theme work. I decided to concentrate on quality over quantity. Having two little children at the time, I longed to give them something really memorable. I decided to make two large teddy bears that I outfitted with jogging suits, pajamas, and a robe. I even made those wonderful bears little sneakers that took hours to make, and were they ever cute! I then sewed outfits for both of the boys that matched all of their teddy bears' clothes. Although made with love, the bears were, needless to say, a time-consuming project. I remember sewing on the last eye for one bear at three o' clock Christmas morning and then spending Christmas Day throwing up.

Despite my greatest effort, I again felt disappointed, so I decided to abandon the homemade Christmas theme. I learned from the teddy bears that it wasn't wise to try to accomplish such a large task in the month of December. My next endeavor was to start the process in June because I had heard that the key to a good Christmas was to start earlier in the year. This would surely be the answer to my nagging doubts about Christmas, and I wouldn't feel so stressed by the time Christmas arrived. I thought I would be on top of the world by December, but all I accomplished was that I bought *more* things, spent *more* money, and stressed over Christmas even *more*. I was never so happy to see January as I was that year.

In my search for better solutions, I mistakenly thought that between being ultra-conservative and trying to make all my gifts, I had been too frugal. Perhaps I was dissatisfied because there weren't enough presents around the Christmas tree. Feeding into the commercial hype all around me, I succumbed. The answer was that we needed more presents. That was it—my children deserved more treasures!

The next year, I decided to try what a friend's family did. There were nine kids in her family, and their parents stocked up on things all year long—shampoo, underwear, school supplies, winter clothing, and necessities—all for the sake of giving them more presents to open on Christmas Day. My husband and I stashed away all kinds of things so we could give our children more presents than ever before, and when Christmas morning came, they ripped into the multitude of presents with gusto and enthusiasm. But imagine our bewilderment when after opening their many presents, the children turned to us and asked, "Is that all there is?" We had unknowingly fostered greed that Christmas as we discovered that *more* presents only meant *more* greediness, *more* debt, and *more* unhappiness! We had actually moved even further away from a meaningful Christmas.

In my meandering journey, I discovered that personal satisfaction was not found with the mere giving of gifts. Still searching, I came to the conclusion that the key was to provide more Christmas wonder—we needed more ambiance, more of the "trappings" of Christmas that we so often see in advertising and television commercials. The garland-wrapped stairways, the elegant trees, the twinkling lights inside and out—that's what we needed! *More* decorations, *more* parties, *more* food.

To begin this new effort, I hosted a "Christmas Around the World" party. I spent hundreds of dollars on decorations for my home and bought bigger and better lights and a huge artificial tree. I planned cookie exchanges, block parties, and evenings with friends. I wanted my kids to feel the atmosphere of Christmas. We spent eighteen of the twenty-five nights that season hosting parties, attending events, eating out, and celebrating the ambiance that I just knew would give us desired Christmas cheer. Although it was fun to socialize, it was exhausting. Peacefulness and reverence took a vacation that year.

When I began this journey to Bethlehem, I thought that the way would be easy. Maybe it is for some people, but for me it seemed that every time I thought I had spotted that elusive star, it turned out to be merely a reflection that ultimately pointed me in the wrong direction. I never imagined that the voices of the world would distract me so easily.

Not finding the answers that I needed, I searched more diligently, pondering and praying for direction. I read book after book and attended every workshop and class I could find that would teach me the secrets of Christmas. I stubbornly kept trying to get it right, and thankfully, every year gave me another opportunity.

Following my hectic social experiment, I decided that the problem was that I just did not have enough time to fit everything in. I have always struggled with the concept of time (just ask my husband), and if my poor time management really was the reason I was not as effective as I wanted to be, then I would just have to become more organized and time efficient!

Armed with determination, I took a class on how to make my Christmas more organized. We were given a large handout with many pages that promised to help us live a fuller and more meaningful Christmas. There was a page for gift planning—with columns for itemizing gifts, recipients, whether the gifts were to be made or purchased, and the date when they should be wrapped and ready. There were detailed pages to record plans for decorating, cooking, and baking, and even spiritual plans, all with columns to write even the smallest details. There were columns for which ingredients to buy, what meals to plan, and who should help with each task. There were columns to record the time needed to complete each step, where to purchase items, and approximate costs. There was a page for family projects and traditions to be filled out, and a detailed calendar of the four weeks before Christmas so that we wouldn't miss a single moment that could be used for preparation.

I came away from the class feeling defeated and overwhelmed. As I studied my newly acquired guidebook for the perfect Christmas, I felt angry instead of encouraged. Surely the answer couldn't be this! Was I really expected to be this organized, this effective, this accomplished in providing my family with a meaningful Christmas?

If the answer to my struggles was this ultra-organized day planner, then I knew that I might as well just admit defeat. After years of trying to get it right, I had become so dissatisfied with the whole business of Christmas. I absolutely hated the materialism, the busyness, the debt, the expectations, and the lack of the peaceful serenity that I so longed for. Most of all, I hated what was happening to my children. They had become greedy and impatient, and I had done nothing to teach them otherwise. Now it was my turn to ask the same question that they had voiced: Is this all there is to Christmas? My personal journey to find Bethlehem had taken me far too long, and I was becoming a weary traveler.

CHAPTER 2

Bearing Gifts, We Traverse Afar

Along my journey, I realized I was not alone in my feelings. It seemed that everyone else was also looking for answers. I would hear friends and total strangers alike exclaiming how they hated Christmas and how, like me, they were disappointed with everything about it.

Linda Eyre, founder of Joy School, expressed similar feelings in a Christmas newsletter:

> Every Christmas I vow that I'm going to get organized sooner by having all my presents bought by December 1. I commit myself to quit accepting assignments to take special treats to the fourth grade when I don't even have time to make Christmas cookies with my own children, and resolve that I'm going to quit worrying about what clever new things to take to the neighbors. None of which I do with much success.
>
> I had begun to feel that I was not in control of Christmas; Christmas was in control of me. I was on a merry-go-round that demanded toys and gifts for everyone. Dozens of people needed to know of our love through a clever or handmade gift, not to mention the food, family parties, church parties, friends' parties, and kids' Santa Claus lists. The list went on and on and made me tired just thinking of it.

I became especially alarmed last year when I heard several mothers with large families say, "I hate Christmas. It is really the low point of my year." I must admit that I have had that very thought cross my mind.[1]

Expressing similar concerns, Brother W. Jeffrey Marsh stated the following in an online magazine article: "'Bah, Humbug!' Ebenezer Scrooge's dour attitude about Christmas begins to settle in on many people's hearts when they see Christmas decorations going up as early as Halloween. Feelings of dread often accompany the 'making of lists, and checking them twice' in order to make certain nothing is left undone for Christmas. So many obligations! So much to do! And so much of it has become so commercialized! How is it possible to live in 'tinsel town' and feel the real Spirit of Christmas?"[2]

If we are honest about our feelings, most of us would admit to having similar resentment and frustration about this season that should be the most satisfying time of the year. Most of us feel stressed and worn out during the Christmas season, leaving us with little energy to appropriately celebrate the Savior's birth.

I have observed that nearly all of the resentment we feel at Christmastime comes from three different areas of concern: materialism, commercialism, and busyness. When any of these words are even mentioned, the response is almost always the same—these three traps are ruining our Christmas celebrations. Yet so few people know what to do about them. It's as if we are battling a force far too large to be reckoned with. Analyzing the depth of my own feelings about the "big three" helped me understand the specific things I abhorred and gave me the courage to try to change those things.

THE TRAP OF MATERIALISM

Wealth and materialism are not new to our day and age. We know that in the Book of Mormon there were periods of peace and prosperity, followed by worldliness and the resultant pride that brought about the downfall of societies. Jacob, brother of Nephi, spoke to his people about their pride that resulted from wealth:

> Wherefore, I must tell you the truth according to the plainness of the word of God . . . that many of you have begun to search for gold, and for silver, and for all manner of precious ores, in the which this land, which is a land of promise unto you and to your seed, doth

abound most plentifully. And the hand of providence hath smiled upon you most pleasingly, that you have obtained many riches; and because some of you have obtained more abundantly than that of your brethren ye are lifted up in the pride of your hearts. (Jacob 2:11–13)

After the Restoration, wealth continued to be a concern. President Brigham Young prophesied to the Saints shortly after arriving in the Salt Lake Valley that the people of the Church would have to endure a trial of wealth and materialism. "The worst fear that I have about this people is that they will get rich in this country, forget God and his people, wax fat, and kick themselves out of the church and go to Hell. This people will stand mobbing, robbing, poverty and all manner of persecution, and be true. But my greater fear for them is that they cannot stand wealth . . . and yet they have to be tried with riches, for they will become the richest people on this earth."[3]

We are told that this land of promise was blessed and reserved for the sake of the Lord's work, but only if we use this blessing of wealth in a righteous way. President Spencer W. Kimball told us: "Do we have more of these good things than our faith can stand? . . . Forgotten is the fact that our assignment is to use these many resources in our families and quorums to build up the kingdom of God—to further the missionary effort and the genealogical and temple work; to raise our children up as fruitful servants unto the Lord; to bless others in every way, that they may be fruitful. Instead, we expend these blessings on our own desires."[4]

He also spoke of this at the dedication of the Washington D.C. Temple: "Bless all people, our Father, that they may prosper, but not more than their faith can stand. . . . We pray that they may not be surfeited with flocks and herds and acres and barns and wealth which would bring them to worship these false Gods."[5]

Despite President Kimball's pleadings, we have been blessed—no, *tried*—with prosperity to see if we will stand on the Lord's side. But if we cannot use our resources to help those who are in need at Christmastime, when our hearts are softened and turned to Him more than any other time of the year, then we stand in danger of failing this crucial test of our faithfulness.

THE TRAP OF COMMERCIALISM

Many years ago, the following questions were asked in a *New Era* article: "Can we let the values, customs, and practices of the world determine how we observe or commemorate such an important time as Christmas? Is there a better way? What should be different about a Mormon Christmas?" Sister Helen K. Richards, wife of Elder Franklin D. Richards offered this response:

> Hasn't Christmas gotten a little out of hand? Haven't the merchants, advertisers, promoters, and others who profit financially taken over pretty much? Do you feel good about this? I don't, and I don't think our Heavenly Father does either. What should be a holy day filled with peace and love and goodness has become a mad scramble of presents for everyone, especially those who will be giving presents to you, decorations, Christmas trees, big feasts, parties, all the material and worldly practices that have almost completely eclipsed the real meaning of Christmas and have little or nothing to do with it.[6]

Economists tell us that our country has evolved from a goods and services economy into a consumer society. We want and insist on having everything that we see, even when those things are beyond our means and we must go into debt to obtain them.

Although today's parents were raised with the values of thrift and self-sacrifice, today's kids are growing up in a culture that demands instant gratification, and they will face even greater trials due to the "gimme-gimme" consumerism of today's and tomorrow's society. They want much more because there is so much more out there to want.

According to the Federal Trade Commission's Bureau of Economics, every year children watch more than 25,000 television advertisements about the latest and greatest products on the market. That does not even take into account product placement on the Internet, video games, and fast food promotions aimed at children. Corporations relentlessly target children, shamelessly commercializing their childhood.

Our children have become the most brand-conscious generation ever. Having a pair of jeans with a logo attached to it is not all that threatening or dangerous, but advertising sells children on more than just products and brands. According to the American Academy of Pediatrics, advertisements contain viral marking techniques that are designed to take advantage of children's friendships by encouraging them to promote products to their peers. As if peer pressure is not enough of an obstacle already! Marketing also exploits older children's desires to fit in with their peers and to rebel against authority figures as a selling point for their products. And these ploys are increased to take advantage of children's Christmas lists and desires.

It is important for us to educate ourselves about the harmful effects of commercialism, as it also promotes attitudes and behaviors that have the propensity to eat away at the very core of our family values. Too much exposure to advertising can lead to violence, aggression, poor self-image, dieting, obesity from fast foods, substance use and abuse, and a distorted understanding of normal sexuality.

One of the most covert lies that advertising has perpetuated is that too much is not enough. At a session of BYU Women's Conference, Mary Ellen Edmunds, a popular LDS speaker, shared this humorous observation: "You can never get enough of what you don't need. Ever. What you don't need never satisfies. . . . We spend money we don't have to buy things we don't need, to impress people we don't like, who don't come over. So here you are, paying bills for the stuff you really didn't need and really couldn't afford to impress friends you really don't have, and no one's there getting jealous! It ticks me off!"[7] Sister Edmunds has a such pleasant and effective way of making us see ourselves in a different light while still helping us laugh about it.

All humor aside, the truth is that we have been subtly deceived by the adversary into believing that if we are unbridled in our generosity to our children, we are giving them an advantage in this world. The notion that the more children have, the more successful they will be is a lie perpetrated by the father of all lies.

The belief that we have to shower our children with everything they have ever wanted creates a problem for parents who struggle to make ends meet. These parents can easily become victims of guilt and sorrow because they can't give their children what they think their children deserve. This leads to a choice of either depriving their children of their happiness or going into debt to fulfill their wishes.

And for those parents who have been blessed financially, it has never been more difficult to avoid the allure of more things. Parents have a hard time saying no when they have the financial means to say yes. The struggle to set limits has never been tougher, but the stakes have never been higher, and they are not just economic in nature.

In his book *Overindulged Children*, Dr. Jim Fogerty, a well-known therapist in the field of parenting, states that overindulging children may seem harmless but can be hazardous. He explains that these children grow up to be angry, resentful, and indifferent. As teens, they grow distant from their parents, demonstrating love only when their parents give them what they want (and becoming angry and resentful when their parents don't). "Overindulgent parents love their children," Dr. Fogerty adds, "but overindulged children do not love their parents."[8]

Giving our children too many things fosters a disrespect of things and people and creates developmental delays in their emotional and spiritual growth. Overindulged children tend to have an inflated sense of self and never seem to learn the most important lessons about the gospel—that every individual can be of service to others and that life has meaning beyond one's own immediate happiness.

Our children will be expected to endure much opposition, and we must consciously choose not to be willing contributors to it. Instead of giving them material goods, we should give our children armor to protect themselves from the adversary. We need to teach them to be selfless, and there is no better time to do that than at Christmastime—but only if we can resist the temptation to indulge ourselves and our children.

As parents, we must strive to be better examples by modeling self-control and moderation. We must guard our own hearts against materialism and greed in order to safeguard our families against its devastating effects. We need to live our lives centered on higher values in order to have the credibility to teach those principles to our children. They include delayed gratification, hard work, personal accountability, honesty, compassion, and moderation in all things.

It is difficult to teach these values in a society that puts more emphasis on the acquisition of things than the building of honorable character traits. If we are watching these outward signs, we understand that they are indications that we are living in the last days. We read in Doctrine and Covenants 45:26, "And the whole earth shall be in commotion, and men's hearts shall fail them." Some argue that this scripture refers to the prevalence of heart disease, but in the next verse we read, "And the love of men shall wax cold, and iniquity shall abound." When charity and love no longer have place in our lives, when we cannot reach out beyond our own needs and desires, then our hearts fail us. Greed is rampant in our day and age, and it causes men's hearts to harden and fail in much more eternally damaging ways than heart disease.

Recently I watched a documentary about how out-of-control consumerism has become during the Christmas season. I was truly disturbed as I watched the scenes of crowds in stores, fighting one another over the latest techno-gadget or loss leader that had been heavily promoted to attract hoards of people. It reminded me of John's description in the book of Revelation of the worldly conditions prior to the Second Coming of the Savior. John tells us that people in the latter days will become as locusts and scorpions upon the earth. The documentary was a visual unfolding to me of this revelation, as I watched people descending in countless numbers like locusts and consuming everything in their path. They fought like scorpions poised with venomous tails, ready to lash out at the nearest offender.

I'm certain that shopping on Black Friday and other evidences of out-of-control consumerism are not the only indications that John's revelation is being fulfilled in our day. There are many signs of locust and scorpion behavior in our society, as evidenced by reality TV shows that portray vindictive, venomous behavior of people lashing out at each other in emotionally and physically destructive ways. But the documentary was a strong reminder to me of how vigilant we have to be to ward off Satan's tactics of unabated consumerism and greed that threaten to permeate the sanctity and safety of our homes and families.

THE TRAP OF BUSYNESS

One can hardly address materialism and commercialism without mentioning the resultant busyness that they create. They are so tied together because shopping for numerous presents and material goods takes an incredible amount of time, as does extensive decorating, elaborate baking and cooking, planning parties, and hustling to fill every moment of the season with some activity.

Life is busy enough with all of the cooking, cleaning, driving children around, careers, church responsibilities, and all the ordinary things that parents have to do each and every day of the year. Yet, we expect to add all sorts of Christmas activities to our already overloaded schedules.

The need to manage our time effectively is the hallmark of our generation. Elaine L. Jack, a former Relief Society general president, said,

> Time is a critical issue for women today. There are sisters in the Church who spend half the day, every day, bringing water from wells to their homes. That's how they have to spend their time. They never have a day off. There are sisters who stand in line for hours to buy scant supplies of food. There are sisters who work in the fields all day

to earn enough to feed their families. Time is a precious resource we have been given.

I am so concerned about the pace we have set as women in *this part* of the Lord's vineyard. We have automatic sprinklers and taps with running water, hot and cold. We think the many labor-saving devices we have should remove all stress from our lives, but we fail to take into account that it's how we *feel* about what we do that is most important. . . . It seems that the welfare of our own souls is being put at risk as we rush to live all seasons of our lives now. And on fast forward.[9]

If we feel that standing in line for hours to provide food for our families is an appropriate use of our time, then our time is sanctified. But if we look at the other extreme of how we spend our time rushing around, stressing ourselves and wearing ourselves thin during the month of December, then maybe we need to re-evaluate whether or not it is worth the risk.

We will always have to face the consequences of our choices, and the consequence of being too "time-consumed" with the things of this world is that we sacrifice the truly important things. In trying to use our time wisely, we ultimately end up losing the most important time—which is time spent enjoying our family.

"What if," Sister Edmunds tells us, "we are inundated with so many choices: what to read, what to wear, what to watch, what to eat, where to surf on the Internet that we are left with not enough time for the scriptures, prayers, pondering, and attending the temple. One way to interfere with our agency would be to give us too many consuming choices."[10]

A key concept in economics is the law of opportunity cost. Cost is usually measured in monetary terms, but it also applies to anything that we consider of value. Basically, opportunity cost refers to the cost of allocating resources to a particular use—it is the cost of having one thing and not the other. For instance, if I had one dollar that I could spend on either a soda or a bag of chips and I choose to buy a soda, my opportunity cost would be the bag of chips. My soda would cost me a dollar *plus* anything else I might have purchased if I hadn't spent it on soda. My purchase cost me the *opportunity* to spend that amount for something else.

In all matters regarding the use of our time, energy, or resources, we are subject to this law. It's a matter of choice, and the opportunity cost is the relinquishing of one choice over another. It is the cost and consequence of our decisions. Simply put, the time, energy, or resources that we expend on one thing cannot be spent on something else.

Every moment that is spent in searching, buying, storing, and wrapping presents is one moment less that we get to spend in more meaningful time with our families—the opportunity cost is the time that could be used creating memories, teaching valuable lessons to our children about the Savior, and serving one another.

Too often we rush around, becoming stressed as we try to do everything, be everywhere, and please everyone. In essence, we think that rushing is a necessary part of life. Darla Isackson, one of my favorite authors of the online *Meridian Magazine*, offers this sound piece of wisdom:

> How ironic that we spend so many of our December hours following traditions that lead us to celebrate the birthday of the Prince of Peace in such *un*peaceful ways! . . .
>
> Strange as it may sound, I suggest we draw nearer to the Savior and be more like Him this Christmas season by repenting of the habit of hurrying. . . . I was convinced that hurry was righteous. After all, if I hurried couldn't I accomplish more worthwhile things, serve more, read more scriptures, do more for my children? But where had all that hurrying got me? Certainly not to joy and peace!
>
> The Savior never hurried, and if I wanted to be more like Him, I would walk a more peaceful path. Never mind that He had the whole world to save. Jesus ministered calmly to his flock, one by one. Never did he say, "Sorry, but I'm in a hurry," when someone needed Him. And more importantly, He never said, "Hurry and follow me." And for good reason. . . . Think about it. When we allow the pace of our lives to get just plain frantic we are all too likely to end up acting anything but Christlike.[11]

Far too often, we jam our schedules so full of activities that we don't have enough energy left to enjoy all of them. Many years ago, I clipped an editorial cartoon out of the newspaper because it reminded me of myself. It shows a woman in a modern-looking home, apparently in the middle of decorating. Christmas lights, bulbs, and garlands are strewn across the carpet. The woman is answering the door, where Joseph is standing and pointing to Mary on a donkey outside. The woman is saying, "You caught me at a bad time—I've got shopping to do, gifts to wrap, lights to put up, a tree to trim, cards to send off, cookies to bake, people to have over, and Lord knows how many Christmas parties to attend."

The irony of this cartoon was not lost on me. Even though the times we live in are busy and hectic, we still seem to find the time to do everything that we really want to do. But with all that we are trying to accomplish, when that knock comes to our own front door, will we be too busy to answer it? Or will we unwittingly sabotage our deeply held beliefs and send that young couple on their way?

In Luke 2 we read, "And [Mary] brought forth her firstborn son, and wrapped him in swaddling clothes, and laid him in a manger; because there was no room for them in the inn" (v. 7). The signs were there—subtle but present nonetheless. In my rushing around trying to do everything I felt was demanded of me during the busy Christmas season, I had inadvertently placed a "No Room" sign around my heart and my home.

The late Reverend John C. Livingston stated it this way: "How strange is the satire that we who spend the most at Christmas, who sing the most carols, who give the most, who want to exalt Christ the most at Christmas—that we would be the seekers of comfort, the prudent and the careful who would fill the inn to overflowing while the glory of God passes us by!"[12] In dedicating so much of our time and energy on the details of our well-intended celebration of the Savior's birth, we sometimes overlook the reason He came in the first place. I had been guilty of this, and I found the need to repent from my short-sightedness and misguided intentions.

In Jacob 4:14, we read, "Wherefore, because of their blindness, which blindness came by looking beyond the mark, they must needs fall; for God hath taken away his plainness from them." In trying to understand what "looking beyond the mark" means, I imagine that Jacob and his fellow Nephites were skilled in the art of archery, which provided the food essential for their survival. When they aimed their arrows at their targets, becoming distracted and taking their eyes off the mark for even a second would cause them to perish for lack of food.

It is just as essential for our spiritual survival to keep our eyes on the mark, which is Jesus Christ. It's interesting that the Lord uses the symbolism of sight to teach this scriptural analogy. Spiritual sight is the ability to discern truth by the power of the Holy Ghost; it is the power to see with "the eyes of understanding" (D&C 110:1). During the Sermon on the Mount, the Savior said that the "light of the body is the eye; if, therefore, thine eye be single, thy whole body shall be full of light" (3 Nephi 13:22).

Sometimes we have a difficult time keeping our sights focused on that which is essential, and thus we look beyond the mark. We are distracted by the world and put too much of our energy, time, and attention on the pursuit of our temporal desires. Having the ability to discern between that which is eternal and that which is from the world is crucial to our application of the gospel, not only at Christmas, but all the time.

I didn't want to become that woman in the cartoon who turns away the Son of God because my heart had become a busy inn that had no room for Him. During my journey to Bethlehem, I began to understand the effect that worldliness has on the way we celebrate Christmas. Equipped with eyes of understanding and a new sense of direction, I continued on my journey.

Notes
1. Linda Eyre, *Homebase Magazine*, vol. 13, no. 4, 1992, 2–3. Used with permission.
2. W. Jeffrey Marsh, "Symbols of the Savior at Christmas," *Meridian Magazine*, Dec. 6, 2001, http://meridianmagazine.com. Used with permission.
3. Hugh Nibley, *Brigham Young, the Man and His Work* (1936) 128, as cited by Gordon B. Hinckley, "Let Not Your Heart Be Troubled," BYU Devotional, Oct. 29, 1974. See also James S. Brown, *Life of a Pioneer*, 1971, 122–23.
4. Spencer W. Kimball, *Teachings of Spencer W. Kimball* (Salt Lake City: Bookcraft, 1982), 357.
5. Ibid., 354.
6. Helen K. Richards, "What Should Be Different About a Mormon Christmas?" *New Era*, Dec. 1976, 14–16. Used with permission.
7. Mary Ellen Edmunds, BYU Women's Conference, "Avoiding the Alluring Call of Materialism" (BYU Broadcasting, April 30, 1998), archived recording at http://www.byub.org/talks. Used with permission.
8. Dr. Jim Fogerty, as quoted by Sugandha Jain, "Too Much of a Good Thing," *Parent: Wise Austin*, Dec. 2006, http:// www.ParentWiseAustin.com. Used with permission.
9. Elaine L. Jack, Open House Address, March 1995, as quoted by

Janet Peterson, "Doing Something Fine with Your Time," *Meridian Magazine*, Jan. 8, 2009, http://www.meridianmagazine.com. Used with permission.
10. Mary Ellen Edmunds, ibid.
11. Darla Isackson, "Slow Down and Appreciate Christmas," *Meridian Magazine*, Dec. 5, 2006, http://www.meridianmagazine.com. Used with permission.
12. Reverend Dr. John C. Livingston. Used with permission.

CHAPTER 3

we Three kings

During my journey, I inadvertently stumbled onto paths that led me away from Bethlehem. I came to understand that materialism, commercialism, and busyness were nothing but deadend roads, and I was able to clearly discern what I disliked about Christmas and the way it is celebrated.

It has been said that when you want to stop thinking certain negative thoughts, you can't just simply eliminate the thought; you must replace it with something positive. Eliminating the negative is only half of the battle. I was now prepared to set my sights upon the positive qualities of Christmas. It was time to examine the blessings and the goodness of the season under the light of yonder star. It was time to see what could and should be the very best part of Christmas.

One thing I have learned about the gospel of Jesus Christ is that it teaches us correct principles and doctrine, but it is by the Spirit that we learn how to individually practice those principles. *Knowing* what is right is not the same as *doing* what is right. That is why personal revelation is necessary for our eternal progress. It customizes truth so that we can understand it and apply it. All people are unique in their experiences, backgrounds, and cultures, and we all face different challenges and circumstances. We must have a personal road map if we expect to get anywhere on this journey called life.

THE NEED FOR PERSONAL REVELATION

Personal revelation is a great blessing to us. It is the privilege and the right of every member of the Church to receive and enjoy the gifts of the Spirit. In Doctrine and Covenants 42:61, we read, "If thou shalt ask, thou shalt receive revelation upon revelation, knowledge upon knowledge, that thou mayest know the mysteries and peaceable things—that which bringeth joy, that which bringeth life eternal." How wonderful it would be to know the mysteries and the peaceable things of the kingdom. But more often than not, in this world it is more likely that the keys to obtaining the peaceable things of the kingdom remain a mystery.

One thing I do know is that obtaining peaceable things does not come in the midst of chaos. It comes as a quiet breeze through our souls, and it comes to us most often in quiet settings because that's when we are receptive and available. Therefore, it's ironic that at Christmastime, when we truly want to enjoy the "peaceable things of the kingdom," when we desire to be closer to our Savior, we become far too busy to listen.

In his book *That All May be Edified*, Elder Boyd K. Packer tells us, "The Spirit does not get our attention by shouting or shaking us with a heavy hand. Rather it whispers. It caresses so gently that if we are preoccupied we may not feel it at all. . . . Occasionally it will press just firmly enough for us to pay heed. But most of the time, if we do not heed the gentle feeling, the Spirit will withdraw and wait until we come *seeking* and *listening*."[1]

Elder Packer has also told us:

> The world grows increasingly noisy. . . . This trend to more noise, more excitement, more contention, less restraint, less dignity, less formality is not coincidental nor innocent nor harmless.
>
> The first order issued by a commander mounting a military invasion is the jamming of the channels of communication of those he intends to conquer. Irreverence suits the purposes of the adversary by obstructing the delicate channels of revelation in both mind and spirit.[2]

I imagine that Satan laughs when he sees us becoming so distracted by noise and busyness that we jam our own channels of communication with the Spirit. Satan can use our best intentions to bring about our downfall. He is the great deceiver and delights in seeing us traveling down the wrong path!

In 2 Nephi 32:3–5 we read:

> Angels speak by the power of the Holy Ghost; wherefore, they speak the words of Christ. Wherefore, I said unto you, feast upon the words of Christ; for behold, the words of Christ will tell you all things what ye should do.
>
> Wherefore, now after I have spoken these words, if ye cannot understand them it will be because ye ask not, neither do ye knock; wherefore, ye are not brought into the light, but must perish in the dark. For behold, again I say unto you that if ye will enter in by the way, and receive the Holy Ghost, it will show unto you *all things what ye should do* (emphasis added).

The Church of Jesus Christ of Latter-day Saints was founded on the principle of personal revelation. It would not exist had it not been for the revelation that Joseph Smith received as an answer to his prayers. He was seeking and listening. He went knocking, and the door was opened to him. We are entitled to this same gift of inspiration and revelation. In fact, Joseph Smith tells us, "No man can receive the Holy Ghost without receiving revelations."[3]

INVITE THE SAVIOR IN

This desire to know the peaceable things of the kingdom led my husband and me to work together to find more meaning in Christmas. I am deeply grateful to have a husband who wants to live the fulness of the gospel, and I consider it the greatest blessing of my life that we can communicate things of the Spirit as we work together to overcome our challenges and find joy in this life. He has been very supportive of me as we have walked hand in hand, striving to find our way through this wilderness.

As we went seeking and listening, we agreed that our most important desire for Christmas was for our children to personally know the Savior. We wanted the kind of atmosphere in our home that would produce peace and tranquility so that we could celebrate His birth with a fulness of heart. We wanted quality traditions, but we also wanted simplicity and the joyful family unity that comes especially from serving others.

We reasoned, how would our celebrations be different if the Savior came to the Wamsley house to celebrate His birthday with our family? How would we celebrate this joyful event? Would we meet Him at the door, grab His hand, and rush out the door to the mall to spend hours looking for the right present, all the while complaining that we have too much to do? Perhaps we could enlist His help to decorate the twelve-foot tree in the entryway, or to help us carry the thirty boxes of decorations down from the attic. Maybe we could ask Him if He wouldn't mind baking that last ten dozen cookies. Then, maybe we would run off to the ward Christmas party. Who knows—maybe He might even catch a glimpse of Santa there!

Truthfully, we know that we would never treat a personal visit from the Savior so casually. Hopefully it would, instead, be a joyous event where we could reverently bask in the love and the teachings that He has to share with us. It would be quiet; it would be fulfilling and inspiring; it would be life-changing. We would rejoice in all our blessings and would never want to leave His side.

Imagine what it would be like if Jesus were to abide with us as our guest for the entire Christmas season. Just think how that would change the way we spend our time. It is quite a sobering thought!

The story of Mary and Martha gives us a little bit of insight into what it would be like to have the Savior as a guest in our home. We know that both of the sisters were faithful disciples of Jesus and that they both had a strong testimony of His divinity. He visited them in Bethany from time to time, and it was Martha's privilege to offer Him the hospitality of her home. "But Martha was cumbered about much serving, and came to him, and said, Lord, dost thou not care that my sister hath left me to serve alone? Bid her therefore that she help me." (Luke 10:40). An interpretation that we hear often is that Martha was distressed (one definition of cumbered) about having to serve.

As I read this passage of scripture, I don't think that Martha was just complaining about having to work. Another definition of cumbered includes being "over-occupied with cares or business, being weighed down or hindered." I think Martha was "cumbered about," as in *running about*, "much serving." I believe she was pleased to serve the Lord and was doing it in a way that she thought was necessary. There is a lot to do when you have house guests, and she needed help, thus her plea for Mary to help.

"And Jesus answered and said unto her, Martha, Martha, thou art careful and troubled about many things: but one thing is needful: and Mary hath chosen that good part, which shall not be taken away from her." (Luke 10:41, 42) Martha was careful, and in trying to be a good hostess, she was troubled about the many tasks that needed to be finished.

How many times have we found ourselves in this exact position? How many times do women, who have the temporal welfare of our families as a righteous concern, rush around, weighed down by the details of trying to get it all done with too little energy and not enough time? Was it unrighteous of Martha to want clean towels and the floor swept when the Savior came to visit?

I've had many opportunities to be like Martha. I've been too careful and I've been troubled, especially during the month of December. Women everywhere feel that, just like Martha, they end up having to do everything themselves. How many times have we pleaded with members of our family to help with the chores?

We have a tendency to look at Martha as unfocused and unrighteous and to fault her for her choices. But instead of chastising her for making poor decisions, I believe that Christ was complimenting her on how careful she had been to provide for their temporal needs, which is a necessary part of life. The Savior would have been grateful and empathetic—He would have noticed the amount of work that Martha had been doing on His behalf.

But He was also inviting Martha to go beyond the temporal, to do that one thing that was necessary at that moment—leave the cares of the world and partake of the spiritual blessings that He wanted to bestow on her. Mary had chosen that "good part." She had quieted her cares and was focusing on the Lord and His teachings.

The phrase "it shall not be taken away from her" is curious to me. I believe that Jesus was telling Martha that He wasn't going to make Mary leave right then to do the chores. She was where she needed to be at that moment. As the Lord often spoke in parables and in layers of deeper meaning, I believe He was teaching Martha that there is a moment in time, after we have taken care of our family's needs, that obsessing and dwelling on perfection prevents us from moving on to the "good part," the part that has the power to exalt. This was an invitation to Martha to come and be with Him, not an accusation that she wasn't a good servant. She just needed to go one step more.

SEEK THE GOOD PART

Just like Martha, we cannot sidestep our responsibilities and obligations to take care of our family's temporal needs. But once we have taken care of the essentials, then it's time to get on with the "good part." And there is a lot of good in Christmas—we just need to find, by the power of His Spirit, the one thing that is needful for us at this moment in time.

With my self-examination along my journey to Bethlehem, I began to understand my personal need to get on with the good part. If I was going to invite Christ into my home, then I, like Martha, needed to get past the house cleaning and get on with the soul cleaning. I would begin with what I knew to be true and go from there.

I knew what I *didn't* want. Experience had taught me that. And to help me to understand what I *did* want my Christmases to be, I started looking for some road signs along the way that could direct me and keep me safe from accidently straying from the path.

And there were signs—direct, honest, and true messages given to us through the years from the First Presidency and the General Authorities. We should listen closely to what they have to tell us, as their words of inspiration and direction will be as promptings from the Holy Ghost. But like a whisper, the guidance will only come if we are seeking and listening for it, and only if we quiet our lives long enough to hear it.

FOLLOWING WISE MEN

We could say that the First Presidency are the three wise men of our dispensation who have come to worship, adore, and then proceed along their way to testify of Christ's divinity to those ears that will hear. And like the wise men of old, much of the world is unaware of their identity. But we know who they are. We would be wise to heed their counsel as they will surely lead us to the Babe of Bethlehem.

Attending the First Presidency Christmas Devotional (or the live broadcast in the chapel) should be one of our family's most cherished traditions. Going together as a family in church attire will demonstrate reverence and respect to the First Presidency. If you are unable to attend a live broadcast, you can often see a rebroadcast on BYU television stations.

Some wonderful and practical advice has been given to us during these devotionals. As our world becomes more and more turbulent, the counsel concerning Christmas has become more and more specific. If desired, you can access transcripts from past devotionals on the Church's website at www.lds.org and on BYU Broadcasting's site at www.byub.org.

The advice of one of these wise men, Elder Howard W. Hunter, was counsel that I needed to guide me on my path to Bethlehem. He said,

> The real Christmas comes to him who has taken Christ into his life as a moving, dynamic, vitalizing force. The real spirit of Christmas lies in the life and mission of the Master.
>
> If you desire to find the true spirit of Christmas and partake of the sweetness of it, let me make this suggestion to you. During the hurry of the festive occasion of this Christmas season, find time to turn your heart to God. Perhaps in the quiet hours, and in a quiet place, and on your knees—alone or with loved ones—give thanks for the good things that have come to you, and ask that his Spirit might dwell in you as you earnestly strive to serve Him and keep His commandments. He will take you by the hand and his promises will be kept.[4]

This was one of my first directives, my first priority. I needed to turn my heart to God. I needed to stop, ponder, and pray, regardless of how busy December would become. I needed to consider this time as if it were His and it no longer belonged to me. In return, what a great promise: He will take me by the hand and His promises will be kept.

I found many more words of advice as I listened more carefully. President Hinckley instructed us to, "Learn of Him. Search the scriptures, for they are they which testify of Him. Ponder the miracle of His life and mission. Try a little more diligently to follow his example and observe his teachings. Bring the Christ back into Christmas."[5]

Another wise man, President Ezra Taft Benson, had such a love for the simplicity of Christmas. He said, "This Christmas, as we reflect upon the wonderful memories of the past, let us resolve to give a most meaningful gift to the Lord. Let us give Him our lives, our sacrifices. Those who do so will discover that He truly can make a lot more out of their lives than they can. Whoever will lose his life in the service of God will find eternal life."[6]

Yet another wise man, President James E. Faust, said, "At the heart of the message of the Savior of the world is a single, glorious, wonderful, still largely untried concept. In its simplest terms, the message is that we should seek to overcome the selfishness we all seem to be born with, that we should overcome human nature and think of others before self. We should think of God and serve Him, and think of others and serve them."[7]

In these few examples, we have been told that we should turn our hearts to God, to learn of Him, to overcome selfishness, to sacrifice, to serve Him by thinking of others before ourselves, and to put Christ back into Christmas. If we are receptive to these messages, the celebration of Christ's birth can be a time of instruction and inspiration, designed to teach us things that we might not learn in any other way.

When we strip away the false concepts of Christmas—the materialism, commercialism, and busyness—the road signs clearly remind us that the grand purpose and design for Christmas is to testify of the divinity of the Babe of Bethlehem. The Spirit has whispered this to me, and I know it true. But I still needed to be instructed and guided on how to practice this principle.

How could I live my life so that my actions would testify of the Savior? How would I quiet all the excesses that are so prevalent today? Could I be *in* the world but not *of* the world? These were still troubling details, but I felt that the Spirit was beginning to take me by the hand, whispering to me to heed the road signs, to have faith, and He would deliver me from the wilderness of this world.

I know that Christmas joy is not an illusion. It is a gift and it can be ours, but it must come with quiet contemplation and prayer. I was beginning to feel hope and confidence that the Lord would direct me by His light on this journey that I had undertaken. God has given us that Babe in Bethlehem, and I was never more determined to wake up Christmas morning, happy and grateful for the blessing of His glorious gift to me.

Notes
1. Boyd K. Packer, *That All May be Edified* (Salt Lake City: Bookcraft, 1982), 336–37; emphasis added.
2. As quoted by Jack R. Christianson, *Making the Music Decision* (Salt Lake City: Bookcraft, 1995), 26–27.
3. *Teachings of the Prophet Joseph Smith*, compiled by Joseph F. Smith (Salt Lake City: Deseret Book, 1973), 328.
4. Teachings of Howard W. Hunter, ed. Clyde J. Williams, (Salt Lake City: Bookcraft, 1997), 271. See also Howard W. Hunter, *The Real Christmas* (Salt Lake City: Bookcraft, 1993), 6.
5. Gordon B. Hinckley, *The True Meaning of Christmas* (Salt Lake City: Bookcraft, 1992), 6.
6. Ezra Taft Benson, *The Joys of Christmas* (Salt Lake City: Deseret Book, 1988), 13.
7. James E. Faust, *The True Gifts of Christmas* (Salt Lake City: Eagle Gate Publishing, 2002), 10.

CHAPTER 4

FiELD anD FounTain, Moor anD MounTain

With the star in sight, I was beginning to understand my personal role and responsibility as a wife and mother, as a guardian and keeper of our family holidays. Although Christmas is ideally a family affair, women usually bear the brunt of the chaos and busyness of the season. They are the ones who generally have the responsibility of pulling it all together, since they do most of the shopping, cleaning, decorating, scheduling, planning, and so on. It's no wonder that wives and mothers are the ones who become the most stressed over Christmas.

From my observation, most men usually help somewhat with the decorating, at least doing most of the outdoor lighting. Some husbands and fathers take even more of the responsibility and share the load equally with their wives. Some husbands consider decorating for the holidays "their thing" and take the lead. Fathers care about what happens to their families and can become stressed and frustrated from the sidelines as they watch their finances spin out of control, or worry when they see their wives work themselves into a frenzy.

Oftentimes, fathers can be more objective and insightful because they are not so personally invested in the planning. In some homes, the most meaningful traditions are brought about by fathers who see a specific need and fill it. One year, a friend of ours finally put his foot down and declared that his wife was not allowed to use her sewing machine during the month of December because he was so tired of the late nights and endless projects.

I don't want to underestimate the amount of extra work all the supportive husbands and fathers take on during the Christmas season. Nor would I want to minimize the efforts that they go through to make their family celebrations successful. We couldn't do it without them!

For the most part, however, I think that husbands are fairly content to allow their wives to dictate the pace and tone of the season. After all, if the wife is willing to take on all the extra work, why shouldn't she? Husbands want their wives to be happy, and they probably think that's what she wants. So men grant the women the responsibility of making Christmas a wonderful experience for all involved. But now, along with all of the extra chores and work that has become the burden of Christmas, women also have the responsibility of being the entrusted ones. If it doesn't turn out to be a beautiful and wonderful season, they feel it is their fault. And quite frankly, I do not know of a single woman who has not felt the overwhelming burden of that responsibility at some point in time. No wonder so many wives and mothers hate Christmas!

HIGH EXPECTATIONS LEAD TO DISAPPOINTMENT

As I analyzed my feelings about the responsibilities and expectations that I had about Christmas, I asked myself if I had required too much from the season. Were my expectations set too high? It's amazing how much insight a person can gain with a little self-analytical talk. Of course my expectations were too high! But I was a little less certain about how they became so far out of focus. When did this happen? Where did I get the idea that Christmas had to be a certain way? Who made all the rules?

Expectations can be elusive to us, and sometimes they are deeply ingrained in our souls. They lie deep within us, and we don't even realize they are there until they are not met. In the book *Unplug the Christmas Machine*, the authors suggest that it is helpful to analyze our expectations and fantasies about how we celebrate Christmas.[1] They also suggest that we take a moment to imagine the most glorious Christmas we could possibly have—the physical setting, the activities, the surroundings. What type of food would you serve? What kind of decorations would you use? What types of feelings would you experience? Perhaps your perfect Christmas is like a Currier and Ives Christmas card or a Norman Rockwell painting. For me, the perfect Christmas resembles an elaborate commercial with winding stairs and a mantle beautifully festooned with garland, a gloriously decorated home, and the table elegantly set in anticipation of the perfect family gathering. The children are well behaved and reverent, and of course it would not be perfect without joy, serenity, spirituality, and soft music.

After imagining the type of Christmas you would really like to have, the next step is to ask yourself if your fantasy Christmas is different from your typical Christmas. Be honest in your appraisal. How do the two compare? Think about the last Christmas season. How much of your dream Christmas has become a reality in your life?

These authors suggest some of our expectations are not met because too often we base them on fantasy and not reality—realities such as crying babies, bored teenagers, dirty dishes, and bills that have to be paid.

Sharon Hanby-Robie, author of the book *A Simple Christmas*, states, "Somehow, over time, Christmas has turned into a holiday machine that seems nearly impossible to turn off. What was once an intimate and precious experience has turned into a blaze of lights and unrealistic expectations. . . . The reality is that unless we develop realistic expectations about the holidays, we will continue to be stressed and disappointed with the results."[2]

I believe that whenever people are dissatisfied with Christmas, it is always because of their unmet expectations. Candy Paull, author of *Christmas Abundance*, says,

> [Depression] comes from all the pressures to perform and the unmet expectations of a "perfect" Christmas that isn't humanly possible to achieve. The images we see of happy families cheerily getting along together over a plump roast goose and groaning table may not be our personal reality. Instead, we often find ourselves with overburdened time schedules, family arguments, tight budgets, travel disasters, and loneliness.
>
> Christmas can be especially poignant after the loss of a loved one, when every tradition renewed cries out that the loved one is no longer here to share the joy. The heart aches with the difference between the happy image and the painful reality.[3]

As I began to make an honest appraisal of my own unmet expectations, I realized that the standard by which I judged all Christmases had its early beginnings when I was twelve years old. My father was in the military, and we were living in Verona, Italy, a city alive with history and personality. I was not raised as a Latter-day Saint, so we had very little religious training in our home.

While living in Verona, the deep devotion that my Italian neighbors had for religion touched my soul. I remember longing to know that God was there for me and that He knew me. Searching, I frequented the grand and beautiful cathedrals and churches of Italy and even attended catechism for a while. But as hard as I looked, I could not find Him there.

I attempted to pray, but I really didn't know how to go about it. It seems almost humorous to me now, but I reasoned that I needed to get nearer to Him so He could hear me. So, in my youthful innocence, on a quiet foggy day late in November, I went deep into a field in the Italian countryside. I climbed up into a persimmon tree—its outstretched branches seemed symbolic to me of my need to touch heaven—and I cried out loud and asked God to please let me know if He was there. Despite my pleading, I came down from that tree disappointed that I had not received an immediate answer.

Shortly after that came a December night when I couldn't sleep, my mind reeling with thoughts and excitement of the season. The house was still, and everyone else was fast asleep as I quietly slipped into our living room. I turned on the lights of the Christmas tree and reached for the Bible that my mother had given me for my birthday a few months before. Although I knew very little about the scriptures, I searched until I found the story of the birth of Jesus Christ, which I reverently read as I lay under the lights of the tree.

What followed was an outpouring of the Spirit as it spoke to me of truth, a testament that the little child born of Mary was the Savior of this world. The conviction of heart that came to me felt like it would consume me, and I knew that Jesus Christ was born for me. This spiritual manifestation was personal and very real, and I had received an answer to my prayers that I will never forget. He had suddenly become *my* Savior.

After all these years, I realized that my core belief about Christmas was that it could bring feelings of profound spirituality and joyfulness.

All this time, I had been trying to duplicate those feelings, but they had eluded me. I kept trying to have these meaningful Christmases without realizing exactly what I expected.

I found that we often expect the entire Christmas season to be perfect, that we won't experience any bumps in the road, and that the ride will always be smooth. But we need to understand that as imperfect beings, it is impractical to expect perfection. But we *can* have pockets of peace, moments of perfection, and times of spiritual enlightenment.

I read somewhere that there are two ways to deal with unmet expectations—you either have to adjust your expectations, or you have to adjust your reality to meet them. Either way, you have to take some type of action to resolve the emptiness that unmet expectations can leave in your life.

It is sometimes difficult for us to relinquish our fiercely held desires and expectations. We feel that we deserve to have them met, without ever questioning *why* they should be. We need to turn realistic, to let go of our past tendencies, and to allow the Lord to lead us to where we should go, not only at Christmastime but always.

I once heard a story about a group of men who devised an interesting system to capture monkeys in the jungle. The goal was to take the monkeys alive and unharmed for shipment to zoos in America. Nets would injure the animals, so they came upon a more humane way to capture them. They would use heavy bottles, with long narrow necks, and into each one they put a nut that the monkeys were particularly fond of.

The monkey, attracted by the aromatic scent of the nuts, would come to investigate. Putting his hand into the bottle, he would grab the nuts but could not get his hand out of the bottle because his little fist, with the nut inside, was now too large. The bottle would be too heavy for them to carry away, so the monkey became trapped.

When the monkeys saw their captors, they shrieked and scrambled, trying to escape. But as easy as it might be, they would not open their hands and let the nuts go.

We may smile about how foolish they are, but people often hold onto worldly treasures as tenaciously as the monkeys hold onto the nuts in the bottles. Oftentimes, when we have developed a taste for the things of this world, no amount of urging can persuade us to let go. And if we spend all our time, energy, and resources building something worldly to hang onto, then Satan succeeds in capturing us in his own cunning trap.

Distorted expectations are one of the most common maladies of our Christmas celebrations. The answer is to become realistic and begin to see eternity in its true perspective so that we will not be like those who "were not willing to enjoy that which they might have received." (D&C 88:32) We need to leave the world behind; to be in the world, but not of the world, and we would do well to heed the counsel from D&C 25:10: "And verily I say unto thee that thou shalt lay aside the things of this world, and seek for the things of a better." Our families will be greatly blessed for our efforts, and the blessings will far outweigh the cost of having to give up worldly perspectives.

Understanding my own expectations and feelings gave me a firm conviction that it was indeed possible for me to obtain the spiritually centered Christmases that I had always desired. It gave definition to what I had wanted all along and allowed me to see without tainted lenses. I had begun the work to put all this knowledge and insight into action.

WE CAN REDEEM CHRISTMAS

I think that I had been waiting all along for someone else to take the lead, for someone to tell me exactly how to transform my Christmas. Maybe I was waiting for a law to be passed that would prohibit shopping in December. I had even hoped that the Church would make a proclamation that would define exactly what I needed to do.

That didn't happen, but I had been given this scripture:

> For behold, it is not meet that I should command in all things; for he that is compelled in all things, the same is a slothful and not a wise servant; wherefore he receiveth no reward.
>
> Verily I say, men should be anxiously engaged in a good cause, and do many things of their own free will, and bring to pass much righteousness; For the power is in them, where they are agents in unto themselves. And inasmuch as men do good they shall in nowise lose their reward. (D&C 58:26–28)

The power was within me, and I could make the kind of changes that we needed. In waiting for someone else to rein in my Christmas for me, I had become far too passive in making decisions about something that ultimately was very important to me. It was time to take a more active stance against selfishness, greed, and materialism. I had a conviction that even the smallest choices would impact our home and the spirit we felt.

I began to understand that I needed to be proactive and realize that, as the saying goes, "if it is to be, it is up to me." Sharon Hanby-Robie emphasizes this point as she tells us, "If Christmas becomes lost in meaningless jingles and commercial hype, it is because we let it happen. It is only by choice that we can redeem Christmas. Reclaiming Christmas is not about simply placing a crèche in the town square. Christmas must be redeemed first and foremost in our hearts."[4]

Darla Isackson says it this way: "We always have a choice, we always have options. It really is up to us how we choose to spend each precious minute, and whether we buy with our mint of time what matters the most to us, or what matters least."[5]

I was ready to reclaim Christmas because I desperately needed it. I knew that I needed courage to make the changes I wanted, and I knew that it wouldn't be easy at first. Sister Richards had stated that in her *New Era* article about how Mormon Christmases should be different: "What can we do? We can do many things. We can simplify and make it more meaningful, but I warn you, *it will take tremendous strength to withstand the pressures.*"[6]

She was right—it's not easy to swim against the tide, to do things in new and inventive ways when everyone around you wants you to conform to their expectations. But "fresh courage take"! We *can* go in a new and different direction. We *can* forge a better way. We can be in the world and not of the world!

We can embrace all the joy that comes our way. After all, joy to the world is a gift freely given from our Father in Heaven, who sent His son to redeem us. There is no greater gift that we could ask for, and no greater joy could we experience than when we realize that Christ has provided us with a never-ending Christmas. He has given us everything: "Prove me herewith, saith the Lord of Hosts, if I will not open you the windows of heaven, and pour you out a blessing, that there shall not be room enough to receive it" (Malachi 3:10).

As I contemplated our Father's blessings and these promises, I began to internalize the truthfulness of the Lord's words. I realized that He has given us the agency and the power to choose the manner in which we celebrate not only His life and teachings, but His birth as well. "For the power is in them, wherefore they are agents unto themselves!" It suddenly became clear to me that my choices about Christmas could and should be different from the world's. I do not have to be limited by anyone else's choices if I choose to walk a different path. I am only limited by my insight, my time, and the creativity that I choose to invest in this endeavor. The freedom to choose for myself, my agency, is the gift that Heavenly Father gave to me when He gave me His only begotten Son.

I had received guidance from that star of wonder as it brightly lit the path before me, and I finally understood. I had been over field and fountain, moor and mountain, and at last I had discovered the way to Bethlehem!

Notes
1. Jo Robinson and Jean Coppock Staeheli, *Unplug the Christmas Machine* (New York: William Morrow and Company, Inc., 1991), 117–24.
2. Sharon Hanby-Robie, *A Simple Christmas* (New York: Guideposts Books, 2006), 8, 23. Used with permission.
3. Candy Paull, *Christmas Abundance* (Nashville: Thomas Nelson, Inc., 2000), 59. All rights reserved.
4. Sharon Hanby-Robie, Ibid., 9.
5. Darla Isackson, "Slowing Down to Do What Matters Most," *Meridian Magazine,* April 25, 2006, http://www.meridianmagazine.com.
6. Helen K. Richards, "What Should Be Different About a Mormon Christmas?" "Q&A: Questions and Answers," *New Era*, Dec. 1976; emphasis added.

PART II

6 STEPS TO A MORE MEANINGFUL CHRISTMAS

*O star of wonder, star of night,
Star with royal beauty bright,
Westward leading, still proceeding,
Guide us to thy perfect light.*

CHAPTER 5

Star With Royal Beauty Bright

As I traveled on my journey, many new paths were laid before me, and I learned many new lessons while following yonder star. I had been moved and inspired to look upon Christmas in a new light, and that light—the star—ultimately led me to experience the joys of Bethlehem.

To summarize how we feel often feel about Christmas, a columnist in a Northern Utah newspaper said the following:

> It is quite clear that many of us don't enjoy the holidays as much as we might, because the 'wants' have gotten out of hand. Somehow we have made the holiday or the family tradition too big, too expensive and too time consuming, especially when focusing on the material end of things, insomuch that we end up feeling overwhelmed, feeling poor, feeling used, and feeling tired, so much so, that we have a tendency to throw out the baby with the bath water (an old saying, meaning we get rid of the good stuff as well as the bad).[1]

I confess, I had often felt this way as I journeyed to find the answers that would help our family become content with Christmas. And I am pleased to say that we saved that baby! But it didn't happen overnight. Instead, truth came step by step and line upon line as the Spirit taught me how to put into practice the truths that I had felt in my heart. We have indeed been blessed by the journey.

As I looked back on my progress, I realized that there were six definite steps that I had to undertake in order to create meaningful Christmas celebrations. These steps help articulate our goals and outline our progress, and I believe that they will allow anyone who uses them to have a more meaningful Christmas. They are as follows:

1. Simplify Gift Giving
2. Give All Year
3. Create Meaningful Family Experiences
4. Serve One Another
5. Teach with Symbolism
6. Enjoy Quality Traditions

As with any journey, the first step usually requires the most direction, effort, and attention, and has the most potential for affecting our lives. This is how it is with simplifying our gift giving. Once we have accomplished this, each successful step will take less and less effort because now our compass is pointed in the right direction and we can pick up our pace.

By following step 2, we will reinforce the concept that we can give good gifts throughout the year if we adopt a new method of giving from the heart.

Step 3 helps us understand the necessity of finding time to create uplifting and enriching activities and experiences that will solidify wonderful family memories and bond us together as families. We will be able to focus on what we do together instead of what we buy for one another.

Serving one another, step 4, relates to step 1 because we will not find the time or the inclination to serve anyone until we can simplify the greatest tug on our time, which is gift giving. Service relates to step 2 as well because as we give more gifts of the heart throughout the year, we will enhance our opportunities to serve, which will then translate into the ability to have even more meaningful Christmases because we become accustomed to serving. Serving one another also relates to step 3, having meaningful family experiences, because the very finest of family experiences comes from serving others as a family.

Step 5, Teaching with Symbolism, allows us to use the icons of Christmas to reinforce and teach correct principles about the birth of the Savior and what it should mean to the world.

Although having quality traditions is very important to families, this is the last piece of the Christmas puzzle to put into place. As we progress through the other steps, we will find that we have created for ourselves the most important traditions as an added benefit of following the other steps. We are then free to add unique and individualized traditions that add just a little more fun and enjoyment to our time together.

Using these six steps will allow us to eliminate all the negative behaviors and distractors of the Spirit as we build a foundation for the finest of experiences and memories. In the succeeding chapters, I have gone into depth about each of these steps, with ideas and specific ways to accomplish our family goals. Although I have listed many ideas and possibilities, I am not advocating a larger or busier effort! Even the smallest changes will bring significant results.

Ultimately, I hope that some of these ideas will enlighten, uplift, and give courage to those who, like me, have been looking for answers. It is also my hope that as disciples of Christ, we may move away from the world in the way we celebrate His birth and His life, and find fulfillment and contentment in our efforts, however small they may be.

HOW CAN I START TO MAKE SOME CHANGES?

Family members may resist any changes made to established traditions, especially when it comes to their own presents. However, when children see that changes are being made to unite the family or focus more on the Savior, they tend to appreciate their parents' motives. Children will see that when we make a real attempt to give according to the spirit of the Lord, we give more of ourselves and think more about others. They will feel our sincerity and appreciate our efforts to get into the true spirit of Christmas. And they will notice the difference.

Recently I asked my eighteen-year-old niece what she likes and dislikes about Christmas. To my surprise, she told me that her least favorite part is all the presents. She explained that it always makes her uncomfortable that she and her siblings are "spoiled," and if she could change anything, that would be it. We need to have faith that our children want the same meaningful experiences as we do, and then give them a chance.

To make changes in your extended family, talk with them ahead of time and explain the reasons for the changes you would like to make. This helps to eliminate surprises. Discussing things at family parties or reunions earlier in the year can be helpful, or it may be even necessary to write a letter. You may be surprised and find out that others in the family feel the same way and are relieved to have someone else take the lead in simplifying their load.

It is important that we take the time to reflect on our expectations and our values in order to understand what Christmas should be for us. Husband and wives should sit down and counsel with one another about what they expect and hope for the season. There are questions that need to be discussed, and if there are children, it might be appropriate to have a family council in order to discuss these things:

1. Why are we celebrating Christmas in the first place?
2. What family values do we cherish and hope to teach our children?
3. Do our family celebrations reflect our family values?
4. What gets in the way of doing the things that reflect what is truly important to us?
5. What do we need to change about what we are doing so that our celebrations reflect our values?
6. What do we really like about our family Christmas traditions?
7. What would we change about Christmas if we could?

You may be surprised about how differently family members feel. You may even find out that you have been caught up in the expectations of others outside of your immediate family. As you counsel with your family, remember that children can voice their opinions and give insight, but Mom and Dad need to make the decisions based on what they know is right for the family.

WHAT SHALL WE DO WITH SANTA CLAUS?

One of the biggest controversies among Christians of all faiths is whether or not to perpetuate the legend of Santa Claus. Some people have wonderful memories of Santa and hold fast to the notion that Christmas could not possibly go on without him. On the other hand, others feel that Santa Claus has stuck his round little nose and jolly tummy where it does not belong. Some are so adamant that it becomes blasphemous to even mention the word "Santa" out loud, and they refuse to participate in any gift giving in order to make a stand about their beliefs.

While I neither condemn nor condone anyone else's choices about whether to believe in Santa Claus, I believe that each of us should carefully examine how we feel about him, being guided by the Spirit in order to make this crucial decision. One of the things to consider is how much Santa has changed over the last few decades. He has become far too important for his own sake and demands publicity even when he doesn't deserve it. He dominates our thoughts, our music, our time, our decorations, and even our children's dreams.

When my husband and I were children, Santa Claus wasn't as big an issue because nearly everyone was modest in their approach to gift giving. Although we are comfortable with the choices that we made while raising our children, we fear that our grandchildren face greater harm from adhering to the tradition of Santa Claus than either we or our children ever did. If we had known what a worldly icon he would become, we probably would have asked him to pack his bags years ago for the sake of our grandchildren.

When I think about the role that Santa Claus played in my childhood memories, I remember the year that I first suspected Santa was just a big hoax. It was Christmas Eve, and I waited until everyone was asleep. Then I crept into the living room on my hands and knees, hoping to uncover the truth. I had no more turned the corner when I saw some black shiny boots coming toward me. There was Santa and he was about to catch me red-handed! I hustled back into my bed and threw the covers over my head, hoping that he hadn't seen me.

There was no doubt about it now. I had seen Santa, and no one could tell me he didn't exist—at least not for a couple of years. Then I finally figured out that what I had really seen that night was my dad, who had been away in France for two years on a military assignment. Two years was long enough for me to forget that he wore combat boots. He had been released a month early so he could come home for Christmas, and he slipped in unannounced because he wanted to surprise my mother. I can't deny having a history of believing in Santa, but I certainly don't want to ever be fooled by him again.

THE LEGENDARY GIFT-GIVERS

In trying to make an informed decision about Santa, I studied his origins and history. Sources did not always agree on the historical origins of legends, and sometimes it was confusing to know which source was the most accurate. But the one thing I found to be the most interesting when comparing various Christmas traditions from different places was that most countries and cultures have some type of legendary gift-giver that has been handed down through the ages, and many countries have two or more. Many gift-givers were derived from pagan customs and transformed over the years to represent Christian values.

In the northern European regions, legends are particularly strong. In Germany, where the Catholicism was prevalent, there was the tradition of Father Christmas, an old man with a long white beard who dressed in red. Over time, he was largely replaced by St. Nicholas, and December 6 became St. Nicholas Day. Members of the Lutheran faith preferred the gift-bearer to be the Christ child or Christkindl, but because a baby could not travel from door to door, a young angel was said to deliver gifts on December 25. The legends of St. Nicholas and Christkindl seemed to merge over time and spread to other countries as Kriss Kringle. For Switzerland, it had been Christkindli but now is evolving into Samichlaus. In Belgium, it is Sinter Klaas.

The Swedish celebrate St. Lucia's Day on December 13. In England the legend of Father Christmas has been adopted. In France, there are several symbols of gift-givers. St. Nicholas, protector of children, has his day on December 6, while Pére Nöel (a variation of Father Christmas) comes on Christmas Eve and fills children's slippers with oranges and star-shaped cookies. In parts of France, Le Petit Jesus (the little Jesus) is the chosen gift-giver.

In Spain, the three wise kings bring gifts on Epiphany, January 6. The three kings also bring gifts to children in Puerto Rico. In China, Lan Khoong (Nice Old Father) and Dun Che Lao Ren (Christmas Old Man) are the gift-bearers. In Russia, Berchta is a Christmas witch from the legend of the old hearth goddess. In Italy, gifts come from Bobo Natalie or La Befana on January 6.

The legend of Befana is somewhat interesting. The wise men, it is said, stopped at her home to ask directions on their way to Bethlehem and asked her to join them. She said no, that she was too busy. Later a shepherd asked her to join him in paying respect to the baby Jesus. Again, Befana said no. Later, when it was dark and she saw a great light in the skies, she thought that perhaps she should have gone with the wise men after all. So, she gathered some toys that had belonged to her own baby who had died and ran to find the kings and the shepherd. But Befana could not find them or the stable. Now, each year the tiny, misshapen old woman rides on a broom from house to house on Epiphany, looking for the Christ Child and leaving gifts for the children of Italy.

It is obvious that most people around the world embrace the concept of a symbolic gift-giver, perhaps because it is a way for people to express the truth that all men receive from the Spirit of Christ, that it is good to emulate charity and generosity. The challenge is to relate these symbolic givers to a higher understanding of the Savior, the greatest *gift* and *gift-giver* of all. The question was whether I could use these symbols to teach valuable truths about Christ and how I could weave them successfully into the legends of my own family.

My husband and I had begun to think unkindly of the jolly old man for the symbol of materialism that he had become, and we had tentatively decided that we should probably get rid of him altogether. But we wanted to start our tradition of simplifying our gift giving first, so we postponed the decision about whether or not to kick Santa back up the chimney.

To our delight, we found that with our new tradition of the three wise gifts (see chapter 6), Santa naturally became dethroned. He became somewhat of a rosy-faced delivery boy and never took center stage again. We put away almost all symbols of him in our decorating and replaced any children's books of Santa with more appropriate ones. We made better choices about which Christmas specials to watch and avoided emphasizing him in any way. And it has worked well.

In retrospect, we now realize that we could have been more aggressive and removed him from our Christmas completely. We were afraid our children would be crushed, but I know now that there are far better traditions and many ways to enhance our own celebrations so that he will never be missed. He has become so terribly tainted with commercialism I would suggest that we become more creative in our efforts to give him the boot, so to speak.

WHAT HAPPENED TO ST. NICHOLAS?

Instead of using the Santa that Clement Clark Moore imagined when he penned the poem "The Night Before Christmas," it would make more sense to use the real St. Nicholas as an icon of generosity and giving. President David O. McKay said of him,

> St. Nicholas had the true spirit of Christmas and went about giving comfort to the people and making children happy. He gave gifts but concealed the identity of the giver. . . . To bring happiness to others without seeking personal honor or praise by publishing it is a most commendable virtue. . . . Good old St. Nicholas has long since gone the way of all mortals, but the joy he experienced in doing kindly deeds is now shared by millions who are learning that true happiness comes only by making others happy—the practical application of the Savior's doctrine of losing one's life to gain it.[2]

President McKay was not talking about the modern-day Santa Claus but about a real person who lived in Asia Minor, which is now Turkey. Nicholas was a religious man who dedicated his life to serving

Jesus Christ and became well known for his love of children and his generosity. He was beaten, tortured, and imprisoned in defense of his faith in Christ, but he stood up for what he believed and did his best to apply the lessons of charity taught by the Savior. Unlike Befana, the little old lady in Italy who missed out on her chance for compassion to others, St. Nicholas probably deserves our respect. In Germany, many people still revere St. Nicholas as a gift-giver, but he has no magical powers, no reindeer or elves, and he rides a donkey that he has to coax along. He leaves presents on the eve of St. Nicholas Day, December 6, and this leaves Christmas Day to be strictly a holy day.

Some families celebrate traditions similar to those from Germany, with a separation of the gift giving and holy observations. This is an intriguing idea. You could celebrate St. Nicholas Day as a way of honoring a man who was a real and living icon of giving, a man who knew of Christ and was willing to lay down his life for Him.

I wish I would have thought of this when my children were little, but I think St. Nicholas would make an honorable gift-giver. Parents could tell their children that they are giving them gifts because, just like St. Nicholas, they want to emulate the Savior and give freely to others. Children would understand that the Lord's charity and generosity is reflected by good things that people do.

Children could become "St. Nicks" when they reach a certain age. St. Nicholas tried to remain anonymous. You could be a St. Nick anytime you gave a gift anonymously. You could still maintain a pattern of giving as illustrated by the wise men (see chapter 6 for more details about this) because even St. Nicholas understood the divinity of the Savior. Parents could teach children the truth—there really was a St. Nicholas, and anyone who is charitable and kind and serves others just like he did can be a saint. In this way parents could incorporate the values and ideals of what it means to be a Latter-day Saint.

Families could celebrate gift giving on St. Nicholas Day instead of Christmas Day. Parents would be the gift-givers and pattern their giving to emphasize the gifts given to the Savior. Gift giving would serve to point families toward acts of service and caring motives throughout the remainder of the month, with an eye toward giving back to the Savior, culminating with a religious celebration on Christmas Day.

As a tradition, this would emphasize the positive values of serving, giving, and caring. There would be no competition for our focus and attention because worldly values would not compete with a day set aside for quiet, peaceful contemplation of the Savior. There would be no lies, no make-believe, and no false expectations from children writing long lists of things they are coveting.

Perhaps my brainstorming exercise about how to substitute St. Nicholas as a gift-giver will stimulate the imagination and reinforce the concept that we truly can choose to create traditions that will fill your needs. We don't have to depend upon the "default" application called Santa Claus. We just have to use a little creativity!

SEPARATE THE RELIGIOUS AND SECULAR

One of the benefits of living in Italy was observing firsthand how people could separate the religious and secular aspects of Christmas, which is a practice used in several European countries. Unfortunately American traditions are being incorporated more and more into European traditions, so perhaps things have changed a little bit. But when I lived there, it was inspiring to see how seriously the Italians took their Christmas Day preparations. They didn't give presents on that day. It was preserved as a religious holiday, a time for family, feasting, and reverence for the birth of the Savior. Most Italians had an elaborate dinner and attended midnight mass on Christmas Eve. Their decorations were religious in nature, and they generally didn't have Christmas trees. Instead, every family had a *presepio*, a manger scene that was located in a centralized place where it was admired and revered, and new pieces were added each year. Then, on January 6, they celebrated Epiphany, the day traditionally celebrated as the arrival of the three wise men, and La Befana or Bobo Natalie gave children a few presents. Because the gift giving on Epiphany was in remembrance of the wise men, it felt much less worldly than Santa Claus.

Enthralled by this separation of Christmas Day and the gift-giving traditions, our family thought about adopting an Italian Christmas, except that as a Church, we don't celebrate Epiphany. This holiday was created by the Roman Catholic Church to celebrate the arrival of the wise men and the baptism of the Savior. We understand things a little differently than the rest of the world—that the birth of the Savior really occurred on the sixth of April and that the wise men's journey probably took closer to two years rather than twelve days—and so Epiphany is not something we have embraced.

In my opinion, the intermingling of the secular and religious parts of Christmas is largely to blame for the demise of the Christmas spirit. It makes a lot of sense to leave the world behind when it comes to worshipping the Lord. Although gift giving helps us to emulate the generosity of the Lord, I believe that it should be separated, even if only a little, from the contemplative moments when we joyfully but gratefully consider the meaning of the birth of the Savior.

In fact, worshipping at a separate time than gift giving may just be *the* answer that many are looking for. Spreading the joy out over an extended period of time removes pressure for us to create one large perfect day. Families have every right to make decisions about when and where their gift giving should come, so it is not out of the realm of thought to consider separating the religious and the secular. Just remember, however, that it still would not diminish our need for simplicity and modesty in our gift giving. But it would make it easier to concentrate on the spiritual side of Christmas.

SHARE THE RESPONSIBILITY

After we decide to simplify our gift-giving traditions, we should also learn how to make the most of our Christmas moments by delegating and inviting our families to share in the responsibility of making Christmas a memorable time. We work together so that we can play together! Depending on the ages of your children, you may be able to delegate the cleaning, the decorating, the chores, and the shopping so that one person is not responsible for everything. Your days will be much more relaxed and enjoyable if you can work together.

Delegating responsibilities isn't as difficult as we sometimes think it will be. Everyone is much happier when we establish rules beforehand about who will do what. Moms shouldn't have to spend hours cooking and then have to clean up the kitchen while the rest of the family gets to visit and enjoy each other's company. Make cleaning up a fun process. Do it together, and get it done. Then everyone can enjoy those family moments. You may even want to draw names for chores. Everyone puts their name in a bowl and randomly draws for an assigned task—someone to set the table, bus the dirty dishes, load the dishwasher, wash the pans, dry them, wipe off the counters, take care of the fussy baby, monitor the preschoolers, and so on.

Children can help a great deal with home responsibilities. Our family motto is, "I can contribute to the success of my family." Things may not be perfect, but everyone should have a part in taking care of the responsibilities. It is the time of the year to loosen up a little on our expectations of a spotless house and elaborate decorations. And it's okay!

One year my family built a new home, but I found myself allergic to the new carpet and paint. I stayed in a small apartment while the rest of my family moved into the house just before Thanksgiving. After using filters and cleaning the carpets three times, I was finally able to move in with the family in January. I learned a lot that Christmas. I learned that my eleven-year-old daughter could decorate just as well as I could! I learned that it was really nice to have a break from the task, and I learned to be grateful for the contributions of my other family members. It was an interesting experience to be a visitor to my own home for Christmas. Everyone should have the chance to view their own decorations and traditions as an outsider looking in.

DECORATIONS, DECORATIONS, DECORATIONS

More does not necessarily mean better when it comes to Christmas decorations. I have seen countless blogs with pictures of homes elaborately decorated, and I am amazed at the amount of time and attention these people spend on what essentially becomes an extravagant hobby. I can't even begin to imagine how much time is spent just setting up things. Some have a tree in every room in the house with a different theme. One room holds a country bear theme, another one a peppermint theme, still another, an angel tree. Then there are elaborate garlands, lights, shelves and shelves of collectable statues, and rooms full of Christmas villages. These people would have to spend every moment of their waking time during the season doing this. I don't want to be a Scrooge, but isn't there something more important that we should be doing with our time? What about the law of opportunity cost? How many opportunities to do good have been passed by because of a need to compete for the best dressed home award?

A modestly decorated home and yard are perfectly appropriate for a Christmas celebration, but like most aspects of Christmas, many people take this to the extreme. A woman came up to me after a workshop once and told me that she had been decorating nine trees every year, and three of those were at least fifteen-foot trees. She had been inspired to cut back on her decorating and had decided to decorate only four trees from then on. This was at least a beginning, and I applauded her for moving toward the goal of decorating more simply.

Being modest in our decorating does not mean that we have to eliminate those things that bring us the most joy. But it does mean being judicious in how we use our time and realizing what constitutes an excess amount of energy and time. Anything that is too time-consuming or expensive will detract from the Spirit. Just because we have enough ornaments to adorn five trees does not mean that we have to use them. We can leave them in the box and rotate what we use each year. The key word in any of our activities, decorations, and gifts is modesty, not excess. We should simplify our work, not magnify it!

GIVE YOURSELF THE GIFT OF A DAY

Knowing the amount of time and energy we are willing to spend on things like cleaning, decorating, and cooking helps us keep those activities in line with our goal of simplifying our routines. Every year I try to give myself the gift of a day to do whatever I would like to do. This affords me with the opportunity to personally take in the sights and sounds of Christmas in whatever way fills *my* heart. This has been a tradition for me, and I would heartily recommend it as a way to fill your personal bucket when demands on your time are at their greatest.

One year I chose to spend my day making the garland that I had always wanted for my living room bay window. I collected scraps from several tree lots, went home, and proceeded to make a thirty-five-foot fir garland decorated with lights and some well-placed bows. It was very full and so heavy that I needed help hanging it across the front of the window. It was so simple yet beautiful and it filled my heart. I loved leaving the house so I could see my beautiful garland. Every evening I would walk across the street to admire it. Other people enjoyed it as well, because not a day went by that someone didn't stop by the house and compliment us on the garland. When I measured the amount of time and effort I spent against the benefits that I received from this activity, there was no doubt that this was a worthwhile use of my time—it was my favorite decoration of all time. However, I have not repeated it since because I have chosen other worthwhile activities to do on "my day."

Many people feel guilty taking time for themselves, but I find that giving myself just one day during those first couple of weeks in December empowers me and gives me the enthusiasm to willingly dedicate the entire rest of my time to my family.

BE SELFISH WITH YOUR TIME

We should clear our calendars as much as we can to allow us to have more time for meaningful experiences as a family. We don't have to accept invitations to parties and activities just because we have been invited. I've noticed that successful families seem almost selfish about their family time. They take the time for family activities, they eat meals together, and they have fun together.

Are there any activities we can move out of the month of December? There is no rule that says that you *have* to send out cards. In France, cards are customarily sent to friends through the end of January—just tell your friends that you are French! Or perhaps you would rather send out a newsletter to family and friends for New Year's Day, Groundhog Day, or even Valentine's Day.

Is the week before Christmas the best time to have that large dinner party? Consider the limitations on your time, energy, and money. There are seasons to our lives, and if we don't adapt to our seasons, we may find ourselves "out in the cold." When we have little children, this is the time to celebrate with them, perhaps with a birthday party for Jesus. When children leave the nest, it is comforting to have them return, so having the family party is a worthwhile activity. Fortunately, limitations on our time eventually change, and one day you really might have time to work at that homeless shelter.

Our family started the tradition of having a fun family game night between Christmas and New Year's. Everyone comes for a sleepover, and we stay up late playing games and enjoying each other's company. Everyone can be in their own homes on Christmas morning and New Year's Eve, and it does not compromise the time that parents should be spending with their own children creating their own memories. And because it comes after Christmas, we are more laid-back and ready to have fun together.

We need to prioritize our time, and I don't mean in a hyper-organized fashion with every fifteen minutes in our day planner dedicated to some activity. We don't prioritize just to fit more things in, but to leave more things out! We need to schedule some down time for our whole family and use our energy wisely. And we need to remember who and what is important to us.

Doing that means that we sometimes have to turn down offers and invitations to dinner parties, cookie exchanges, and the like, in order to provide our families with the kinds of activities that will enhance their understanding of the true nature of Christmas. Sometimes, we just have to say "no thanks."

I have never been very good at calculating how long a task should take, or maybe I'm an eternal optimist in thinking I will be able to fit everything I want to do into my meager twenty-four hours. Whatever the reason, I am usually guilty of inadvertently overscheduling my life. I have found that when tasks are left to the last moment, the haste and confusion detract from the Spirit. I have to be deliberate in my effort to allow spare time if I want to be able to live in the moment.

IT IS ENOUGH

It is so satisfying when you know that you are in control of Christmas. It is particularly gratifying to feel that your celebrations are the result of deliberate and thoughtful choices that are yours to make, and that you are not being tossed to and fro on the turbulent seas of commercialism and busyness. Every Christmas Eve before I go to bed, I love to take one more look at our small pile of wrapped presents carefully placed next to the tree. I am once again seized by gratitude that we have chosen to be modest and conservative, not by virtue of economy but by choice.

With a little work and with a little trust in our Father's direction, we can all find this satisfaction on Christmas Day. We should be able to look forward with expectation of a beautiful Christmas to come because we, like the Apostle Paul, can discover that "I have learned, in whatsoever state I am, therewith to be content" (Philippians 4:11).

In Charles Dickens's *A Christmas Carol*, Scrooge returned from his adventures a changed man, with new perceptions about how to celebrate Christmas.

> Some people laughed to see the alteration in him, but he let them laugh, and little heeded them; for he was wise enough to know that nothing ever happened on this globe, for good, at which some people did not have their fill of laughter in the outset; and knowing that such as these would be blind anyway, he thought it quite as well that they should wrinkle up their eyes in grins as have the malady in less attractive forms. His own heart laughed and that was quite enough for him.[3]

His own heart laughed; and that was quite enough for him. Christmas has indeed become a time when my heart rejoices with gratitude that it is enough. Finally, enough has filled my heart, and I am content.

Notes

1. R. Trent Wentz, "Traditions an Important Part of the Holidays," *The Herald Journal* (Logan, Utah), Nov. 14, 2006.
2. David O. McKay, *Gospel Ideas: Selections from the Discourses of David O. McKay*, (Salt Lake City: Improvement Era Publication, Deseret Press, 1953), 550.
3. Charles Dickens, *A Christmas Carol* (New York: Weathervane Books, 1977), 147.

CHAPTER 6

Simplify Gift Giving

The sharing of gifts is one of the most long-standing Christmas traditions. If given for the right reasons, gifts can lighten the heart and bring us joy. But when gift giving gets out of hand, it contributes to the materialism that is so prevalent today.

WHEN GIVING BECOMES A PROBLEM

Gift giving often causes frustration or resentment and sometimes can even cause depression. Some people feel resentful about giving because they can't afford it, or they have gone into debt every year in order to pay for everything. Still others have frustrations about gift giving because they don't enjoy spending time in the stores, or they don't have time for shopping, buying, and wrapping all the presents.

Some people, especially those who are older, don't want any more presents because they are tired of dusting all the knick-knacks in their homes. Still others feel let down and disappointed because they don't receive the type of gifts they really want, even after using all their own resources to please others.

We need to look inward and examine our motives for giving by asking ourselves the following questions:

1. Am I happy about the number of gifts I give?
2. Do I feel that I have an obligation to exchange gifts when I would rather not?
3. Do I feel pressured into giving gifts?
4. Am I giving gifts because someone else expects me to?
5. Do I feel angry about how much money I am required to spend?
6. Who dictates the rules I must follow when giving gifts?

I am troubled when I hear people bemoan how they have to cut back on their presents because of the recession. Apparently, they feel that because they are not giving large and expensive gifts, Christmas cannot possibly be as fulfilling.

Although we have every reason to be troubled about finances, people should not think that their choices for giving are limited because of money. There are far more lofty reasons for deciding on our gift giving habits than how much money we have. The motives of gift giving should never be about money.

One of the most meaningful gifts I ever received was from a friend who, because of circumstances beyond her control, had very little money to spend on gifts. She honored me greatly by giving me the gift of performing twelve random acts of service for others (myself included) during the Christmas season. She understood my desire to serve others, so this beautiful gift was truly one that came from her heart.

Many people have expressed the sentiment that some of their most memorable experiences with giving have come during the roughest of economic times. Childhood memories of Christmases past are so much more often of happenings and experiences than of things. Those who lived through the Great Depression or other difficult economic trials have said that it was in these times that they witnessed the greatest acts of unselfishness. We shouldn't have to experience a recession to learn this valuable lesson.

We should give to one another at Christmas to show our love and appreciation, and our gifts should be symbolic of Christ's gifts for us. If the reason to give gifts to each other is truly about showing our love, wouldn't it make more sense to give our hearts and our time to one another instead?

When we think about these issues, we can understand how giving gifts grudgingly or for the wrong reason is not in keeping with inner peace and harmony, which makes it hard to feel an outpouring of the Spirit. I've found that, like me, most people want to have deeper, more joyful feelings, and they're disappointed when they don't experience them.

CHOOSE TO SIMPLIFY

A columnist for a Northern Utah newspaper stated,

> I have to wonder if the quiet simplicity of the first Christmas wasn't meant to be a test of faith for a world too impressed by noise and glitter. Good things come in small packages, the cliché goes, and there's hardly a smaller or better package than the newborn Savior of the world, asleep in a manger. Maybe God wanted to remind His children that simple can be beautiful; the pure in heart don't need crashing cymbals and sequins to notice what's important. . . . A smaller and simpler Christmas season could be the greatest ever, and leave you with enough time to ponder the gift of the baby born in a Bethlehem stable.[1]

How you simplify Christmas will of necessity be an individual decision. I have a close friend who likes everything about the holidays but gift giving. She is a busy woman with many responsibilities and has little time and few resources. While she feels that she has no choice but to feel tired and resentful, in reality she can make two important decisions.

As mentioned previously, she can alter her circumstances to meet her expectations by choosing not to exchange Christmas presents as a family. In this case, it would work much better if, through prayer and self-examination, this choice is made together as a family. Instead of giving gifts to each other for Christmas, they could do another activity that is meaningful to them, such as a service project, or they could use the money for a family get-together or a mini-vacation. Choosing not to exchange gifts is a perfectly acceptable option. After all, they are making their own rules!

Her second option is to alter her expectations to meet her circumstances. Through prayer and self-evaluation, she can come to understand her own expectations about gift-giving and why they are not being fulfilled. She can learn to change her feelings about the giving of gifts.

For most people, altering their expectations *and* changing their circumstances are both necessary to accomplish their family goals. There are many different ways to simplify, and what works best for one family might not be the right answer for another.

SIMPLIFYING MUST BE THE FIRST STEP

Simplifying gift giving was the first step I needed to take in order to find room in the inn of my heart for the Savior. I needed to pull away from the worldliness that threatened to overtake Christmas, and I learned by experience that this was the most important step I would take in reclaiming the season. If we can conquer this aspect of Christmas, all the other steps to a meaningful Christmas will quickly fall into place.

Issues about gift giving are sometimes difficult to resolve. While it is the first step, it's not an easy step to take. But if we are serious about changing our Christmases, we have to simplify the giving of gifts and it has to be our first priority. I cannot emphasize this enough! We cannot find the time or the inclination to do those things that make Christmas meaningful if we spend all of our time and energy searching for presents all over town.

We should not have to give expensive presents that we can't afford because someone else expects us to. There should be nothing to feel guilty about because giving should be a choice and not an obligation. We shouldn't feel the need to defend our righteous choices. And we do have choices, but in order to exercise those choices, sometimes we just need to simplify and clarify in order to understand what we expect from the giving of gifts.

Most people experience a huge paradigm shift when they change the way they address gift giving. This is a big decision, and we shouldn't procrastinate making it. The increase in our peace and contentment can be a great blessing to us, and the sooner, the better.

HOW WE SIMPLIFIED OUR GIFT GIVING

For my family, the answer to simplifying our gift giving came unexpectedly and was such a blessing to our family. I remembered hearing about a tradition for families to teach children that they should receive only three gifts for Christmas to symbolize the three gifts that were given by the wise men. However, they couldn't just be three random presents. They would need to be more specific to symbolize frankincense, myrrh, and gold. In keeping with the purposes of the original gifts, they would need to symbolize something to amuse, something to use, and something to cherish.

I loved it! It seemed so simple, but it was the perfect tool to put boundaries and limits on our gift giving while emphasizing the events surrounding the Savior's birth. I loved the idea of bringing the symbolism of the first birth into the gift giving, and it seemed to make sense to us that children should not expect to receive more for Christmas than Christ received. We decided to try it, although I was not initially convinced that it would make a lot of difference, since most of what I had tried until then had not been very successful.

To begin, we had a family home evening about the sacred nature of Christmas and how we needed to celebrate it more reverently. We decided to write a letter to Santa Claus and ask him if he could help us have a more spiritual Christmas by bringing three wise gifts to symbolize the gifts to the baby Jesus. As I stated earlier, although we were unhappy with the Jolly Old Elf, we didn't think that we could leave him out in the cold just yet. This seemed to be the best solution, and it worked out wonderfully in the end because he just kind of melted into the background.

It was amazing to see the benefits that this one little change made to our celebration. Defining exact limits for both our children and ourselves brought about impressive results. As parents, we knew that those three wise gifts would have to be chosen carefully, and we almost always knew months in advance what we wanted to give our children. It took insight, the presents came from the heart, and it was nice that it was never about money. Sometimes the gifts that cost the least were the most well-liked. Gifts were tailored to our resources but not defined by them, and it only made the gifts more special.

The average amount of money we spent per child was $75, and the most we ever spent was $125. One year we only spent $30 on each child. That may sound stingy to parents who are used to spending $500 to $1,000 per child, but when you make quality decisions as a family, children seem to understand and appreciate the reasons behind them. They were never dissatisfied with what they received. The gifts seemed to lose all monetary importance as they increased in personal value.

The children no longer wrote letters to Santa, as they seemed to develop a sense of trust that the gifts they would receive would be better than they could ask for anyway. Knowing what to expect from Christmas gave them a sense of security and less anxiety. This helped them be more calm and peaceful during December, and that set the stage for them to enjoy their Christmas activities even more. I was amazed at the difference in their attitudes.

When my oldest son, Daniel, was sixteen years old (a very peer-pressured age), I asked him if he had ever felt deprived when all his friends received more gifts under their trees (which one year I estimated to average between $700–$1,200). I will never forget the sincerity with which he looked at me and replied, "Are you kidding, Mom? We have the best Christmases of anyone I know. Why should I be jealous over anyone else's?"

Last Christmas, our seven-year-old grandson Kason told us about an experience he had at school. Upon returning after Christmas break, one of his friends asked, "How many presents did you get?" Kason replied, "I got three," to which his friend answered, "Well, you didn't get very many! I got lots and lots more than you!" Kason then said with a sense of pride, "Well, if you got more than three presents, then your family doesn't know the right way to have Christmas!" It impressed me how, even at his tender age, he understands that there is a reason for three gifts, and it helps him to see past any need he might feel to have more.

THE SYMBOLISM OF THREE WISE GIFTS

When sharing this tradition, I am always asked to share a little about the things we chose to give that are symbolic of something to use, amuse, and cherish. People have attached many different symbolic meanings to gold, frankincense, and myrrh. One meaning is that the gifts serve as a precursor for the Savior's mission and ministry. Gold symbolizes the crowning of kings, power, authority, and royalty. Frankincense is for divinity because when it is used as incense, its white smoke rises upward to heaven. Myrrh was used to embalm and as such is symbolic of Christ's death and burial. This is only one of the many interpretations and symbolic meanings and it is one that adults can understand.

With children, however, it is much easier to put these things into terms that can be easily understood and remembered. Gold is a precious metal, and it is easy to see how it is something to cherish.

According to Reed C. Durham, Jr., in his book *The Gifts of the Magi: Gold, Frankincense, and Myrrh*, the word *frankincense* comes from the Old French *franc encens*. *Franc* means "pure," while incense (*encens*) comes from *incendere*, meaning "to burn." Thus "pure incense" is the purest and most desirable of all other incense and comes from a balsam-type tree of the genus Boswellia. Its use was intended to bring joy and pleasure to the user, and thus it symbolizes something to amuse.

Myrrh (the root word means bitter because it is bitter to the taste) is from the genus Commiphora and is used to scent ointments and oils for medicinal use and for embalming. Both frankincense and myrrh are gum-resins or sap that ooze out of the bark after it is scored and cut.[2] Myrrh was useful in many substances and is something to use.

Focusing on this symbolism has given our family the opportunity to feel the true spirit of giving. We know that Christmastime is not just for unloading presents but is symbolic of our Father in Heaven's gift to us of His Only Begotten Son. And it is also symbolic of those very wise gifts that were so lovingly presented to Jesus, with a reminder that we too should worship Him in like manner.

Some ideas of "something to cherish" would be a new set of scriptures, a favorite book, a cuddly stuffed animal, a scrapbook of memories, or an heirloom from grandparents, such as a porcelain doll. This category is the most difficult because you really want to give something that will be remembered. Our last "to cherish" gifts were a set of Max Lucado books for our grandson who is living with us and a handcrafted stuffed bear that I outfitted with earrings and a necklace for my teenage daughter.

Examples of "to amuse" are favorite toys or a new computer game. These are the easiest gifts, and the only difficulty I have with this is putting on the brakes and buying only one of the many things I could choose. I also try to limit the size and scope of the amuse gift because we as parents could easily negate the modesty that we are striving for.

Examples of "to use" might include clothing, a new snow tube, a bedroom decoration such as a fun lamp, or an art set. You will always be able to find something for your child to use!

You can see by these examples that you tend to start thinking about what to give, especially to cherish, long before Christmas, so it comes from the heart. I have heard of other people using the three gifts as a basis for their traditions, but there are no definitions or symbolic reminders built into them. Some families choose one large, one medium, and one small gift, and some families choose to give just one gift to each child as a way to simplify. Any way that you can simplify gift giving is great, but I am so thankful to have the symbolism because it never fails to set the tone for a more reverent Christmas.

There is another symbol that we could teach when we use the three wise gifts. Although we know that the wise men came to honor the babe while Joseph and Mary dwelt in a house, it is unknown just how long that journey took. It could have taken close to two years. I read recently that the gifts were precious enough that they would have allowed the young family to escape Herod's murderous rampage and survive in Egypt. It occurred to me that these gifts were symbolic of God's ability to reach out and preserve the young Jesus, who would then one day do the same for us, both physically and spiritually.

One of the great benefits we experienced as parents was that setting limits allowed us to free up our time and energy so we could focus on providing meaningful experiences and service that would elevate our Christmases to a new level. It's important for us to set limits on what we decide to do, and it's important that we stick to them. It takes self-control, but guidelines will help us keep our celebrations in line with our values and will help us when we are tempted to say "yes" when we should be saying "no."

EMPHASIZE GIVING RATHER THAN GETTING

Changing the emphasis from gift *getting* to gift *giving* helps the whole family shift away from materialism. Instead of asking, "What do you want for Christmas?" we should ask, "What are you going to give for Christmas?" or "What surprises are you planning for Christmas?" Then we are in a position to help our children learn about the joys of giving. Planning service projects for our families will also help develop this attitude.

When I think about children and their ability to freely give, I am reminded of an experience that we had with our grandson. When he was three years old, his mom decided to take him to see Santa at the mall. He was excited to go, but when it came time to leave, he refused because he didn't have a present to give to Santa. Nothing we could say could convince him that a gift wasn't necessary, so we quickly wrapped up a new tube of scented lotion (it was all I could find) to give to Santa. Our grandson left carrying that little wrapped box with pride and happiness, and we, including Santa, were all touched by his heart-felt generosity. What a great lesson about what it means to have a giving heart. If only we could all be like these little children!

RECEIVE GRACIOUSLY

When gifts are given from the heart, both the giver and the recipient are blessed. Gift giving is a two-way proposition, and if there is no receiver, there cannot be a giver. However, for most people, it is easier to give than to receive, especially when the gift is one of service. We often need to practice our receiving skills more than our giving skills. Those on the receiving end have the responsibility of accepting the gift with gratitude and without judgment. In Doctrine and Covenants 88:33, we read, "For what doth it profit a man if a gift is bestowed upon him, and he receive not the gift? Behold, he rejoices not in that which is given unto him, neither rejoices in him who is the giver of the gift."

There is definitely an art to receiving graciously when someone lovingly offers us a gift. It's easy to be gracious when we get exactly what we want, but what about the times when we don't?

All gifts, whether wrapped in colored paper or given as an act of time or service, should be of value to us. A handwritten note may even be of more worth than an expensive store-bought gift because it comes from the heart. Even if the item is the wrong size, the wrong style, or just another dust collector, what really matters is the heart of the giver and that he has offered you a part of himself. We don't have to love the gift, only the giver.

My mother-in-law was an example of a gracious receiver. She always appreciated everything we gave her, whether it was a favorite saying painstakingly written in calligraphy for her wall or a simple pair of St. Patrick's Day socks for her birthday.

Although I always appreciated this quality in her, I didn't fully learn this lesson until after she passed away. I had gone to help my father-in-law organize some closets and possessions and was helping him look for her journal when I discovered a drawer in her dresser that contained nearly every gift I had ever given her, many of which I had long since forgotten. I knew her enough to realize that they weren't there solely because she didn't know what else to do with them. But rather, it was because every gift was loved and cherished. My heart was enlarged that day by the great lesson on receiving graciously.

If we are not careful, we could deprive others of blessings by being unwilling to receive their gifts to us. This is especially true of acts of service—a lesson I learned while serving as compassionate service leader several years ago when I asked our Relief Society sisters to take meals to a family who was in need.

I noticed that one particular sister had signed up for the task. I knew that her husband was going to school, they had two young children with one on the way, and they were living in a one-room studio apartment. They were struggling to make ends meet, and her living conditions were less than ideal. I was surprised that she would volunteer for this assignment, when in my estimation, we ought to have been taking meals in to her. Most people would feel justified in not taking a meal to someone else when they didn't have sufficient even for their own family. But when she didn't receive a follow-up call from me, she contacted me. I explained that although I deeply appreciated her desire to help, I had decided to spare her from the obligation.

In response, she wept as she pleaded, "Please do not take away blessings from me that I desperately need! Service is more important to my spirituality now than ever before." Humbled, I arranged for her to take a meal to the family, who later told me that it had been a delicious and most generous meal and that she had given far beyond what they had expected. What a great lesson to learn about the widow's mite. Not only did that dear sister teach me the power of giving, but she helped me understand the importance of receiving and accepting the widow's mite.

At times we struggle more than others, and sometimes we may find ourselves blessed enough to be on the receiving end. We found ourselves in that position one year when we had a choice to buy a few last things we needed for Christmas, including food to last through the month, or to pay our tithing. Having faith that the Lord would provide what we needed, we paid our tithing. The next day, my sister-in-law brought by a one-hundred-pound bag of potatoes, and after that my husband's parents brought us enough cuts of beef to fill our freezer. Then, I needed some stuffing to finish some Christmas presents, but I didn't have the money to buy it. While I was in the sewing room, trying to find some alternative, my neighbor phoned. She had been cleaning out some closets in her house and had found several bags of stuffing. She wanted to know if I could possibly use them. I couldn't believe my ears! This was no coincidence! The Lord had provided for us, and we had everything that we really needed, but He blessed us even more the next day when we received a one-hundred-dollar bill in an anonymous Christmas card.

Being on the receiving end of the Lord's tender mercies allows us to learn gratitude, humility, and how the Lord is ever mindful of our needs. I believe there is as much inherent symbolism concerning the

Savior in receiving as there is in giving. We learn that He is willing to pour out abundant blessings to those who are willing to *receive* them. As the carol says, "Where meek souls will *receive* Him still, the dear Christ enters in" (Oh Little Town of Bethlehem).

LISTEN WITH THE HEART

The best gifts come from the heart. When our grandson's great-grandmother passed away the day after Thanksgiving, Kason (age seven) knew exactly what to do for Great-grandpa. Kason asked us to help him find a picture of Great-grandma and print it so that he could make a card out of it. He then wrote on the inside next to the picture, "I know that she will be with you forever and ever, and I know that she loves you. I love you too!" He was giving everything he knew to give, which was his heart, and it was received with heart-felt emotion.

Time is elusive and gets away from us so quickly. We must listen to the Spirit tell us when there are important gifts to give and when we need to give them. Perhaps it is time for us to get that personal interview from our parents or a special gift that would really touch someone. If we are open to inspiration, we will be led to give these types of gifts that are the greatest gifts of all.

One such time for me was the day after Christmas one year. My sister-in-law had suffered from breast cancer during the year but was doing better. I had a strong impression that I should start immediately on the next year's present, which seemed silly because I was tired of Christmas. I dismissed the thought, but it just kept coming back. I couldn't stop thinking about it, so I came up with an idea for a gift for my in-laws. Because all four children had served missions, I had decided to ask all of them for their mission slides and a narration on tape about the slides, which I would then put onto video for grandparents and siblings. The Spirit persisted (I am grateful because sometimes I argue) and I hesitantly phoned my sister-in-law on New Year's Day to see how she felt about it. I thought she would dismiss the idea and ask me to bring it up again later in the year but she didn't. Instead, she was very enthusiastic and said she would start right away.

She finished two weeks later and mailed me the tape and slides, which I later found out she had kept a secret from her family. Only a few weeks later, Margaret discovered that the breast cancer that she had thought was gone was now in her bones, and in a very short time she was taken from us. As she struggled in those last weeks of her life, she told me how grateful she was to have worked on the project, as it had renewed her enthusiasm for missionary work. She was no longer fearful of death because she knew she had been called on a new mission. Those thoughts gave her a great deal of comfort and peace.

Later that year, my husband helped me complete the project, which we gave to the family that Christmas. Imagine the tenderness in the hearts of her children when they heard their mother's voice proclaim her beautiful testimony about the gospel and her gratitude to be able to serve the Lord. Especially poignant was the message to her husband, whom she had met while on her mission. I cannot put into words the emotions of a grieving husband who wanted so desperately to hear just one more time that she loved him. I'm thankful I listened to the Lord's prompting and was an instrument in providing her with the opportunity to give one last heart-felt Christmas present to her family.

Our Father in Heaven knows who needs His help, and He knows *when* they will need His help. We must keep ourselves in tune with His promptings, and He will give us opportunities to help others that will fill our hearts to overflowing.

This was also the case when the Spirit directed me one year as I struggled to think of the right gift for my father. Nothing seemed right. I wanted to find something special, so I finally decided that I would write him a letter of gratitude. As I was writing the letter, the Spirit made known to me that this was the last Christmas I would ever spend with him. On Christmas morning when my dad read the letter, he was deeply touched, and the tears flowed freely. The next October, he passed away from lung cancer, and I have always been grateful for the prompting of the Spirit to lead me to the right gift.

If we believe that all things are spiritual to God, then we must in turn believe that He who gives us the best gifts will help us know what gifts to give from our hearts. He wants us to give as He would give.

ENJOY THE JOURNEY

One of the traditions that we enjoyed as a family was making the process of opening our presents fun. We were unrushed and took our time enjoying each other's company and sharing in each other's joy. To emphasize the symbolism of the three wise gifts, we would leave off names from the presents, labeling them only with "to use," "to amuse," or "to cherish." We would then number the presents and play a game to figure out who the presents belonged to.

Sometimes Santa (and later Dad) would hide a list somewhere in the room, which a parent would conveniently find, that listed the order we wanted them opened, with "to cherish" usually first. One year, my husband, Jay, wrote the following poem on four slips of paper that the children had to put in proper order to make sense. These were hidden in the branches of the tree.

> Because you have been such fun kids, we are going to play a game.
> The presents are anonymous, they haven't got a name.
>
> Clues are hidden in this room. (Be gentle and don't go crazy!)
> To tell you whose present is whose, and the clues won't be hazy!
>
> So, look slowly and surely, my gentle Wamsley folk,
> And find out who's number 1. Don't get so excited you choke!
>
> Find all the clues, 1 through 12, and lay them on the table.
> Figure them out, open the gifts, singularly, orderly, as soon as you're able.

An example of one of the twelve clues that were hidden was the following: "Number 10: Something to amuse for someone who used to entertain us by stuffing raisins up his nose" (a stunt favored by our son when he was a toddler). Once the clues were found and figured out, the presents were then opened in order by number, one at a time. It was a fun activity and fondly remembered.

We kept the tradition of giving stockings, but we simplified what we put in them, and for many years, it included breakfast (usually a small box of cereal, a banana, and can of juice), an apple, an orange, a pair of socks, and a few little trinkets. I gave my sons a new dollar-store watch every year as a gag gift, and we would see how long it took for the watch to break (which was usually only a week or two).

One of the problems inherent in using Santa as a gift-giver is that sometimes children have a hard time understanding why Mommy and Daddy don't love them enough to give them a gift. Until they are old enough to understand, some parents choose to include one present under the tree from Mom and Dad for the children to open on Christmas Eve, while they await the arrival of the three wise gifts the next morning.

Be creative in thinking of alternative ways to share Christmas with those you love. Invent new ways to do things for others that show your genuine love. For friends, choose to get together and spend an afternoon enjoying friendship instead of exchanging presents. Go on a long walk on a brisk December day, or go out to lunch at a favorite restaurant every year.

Simplifying gifts for extended family members creates a unique challenge. Ask grandparents to help you in changing your family traditions. Let them know your goals, and then brainstorm about possible ideas that you might like to experiment with. Although some might argue, the unspoken rule that you can't dictate how someone else gives you presents no longer applies. We can choose to change anything that does not accomplish our family goals, but sometimes it may take a little time for us to change everything we would like to. But if we know the direction we're going, we'll eventually get there.

Although it is clear that I have a lot of conviction and passion for our tradition of the three wise gifts and the importance of symbolism, I have included many different ways to simplify gift giving in the following pages. Although I have listed many ideas, be careful and prayerful about which ones you choose for your family. Whatever new ideas you may use, remember that simplifying the gift giving is the single most important thing that we can do as families to put Christ back into Christmas.

In the chapters that follow, there are also many examples of meaningful moments that we can spend with our family, teaching them of Christ and feeling of the Spirit, performing acts of service and bonding together as a family. In all of these ideas, remember that too many changes at once could cause stress, and the idea is to simplify, not multiply.

Notes
1. Sally H. N. Wright, "Don't Miss the Point: Celebrate Christmas Simply," *The Herald Journal* (Logan, Utah), Dec. 8, 2005.
2. Reed C. Durham Jr., *The Gifts of the Magi: Gold, Frankincense and Myrrh* (Logan, Utah: Self-published, 1991, revised edition 1993), 5–55. Used with permission.
3. James E. Faust, *The True Gifts of Christmas* (Salt Lake City: Eagle Gate Publishing, 2002), 6.

WAYS TO simplify GIFT GIVING

SIMPLIFY GIVING TO FAMILY MEMBERS

- Children receive three wise gifts for Christmas, one to amuse, one to use, and one to cherish.
- Children receive three gifts for Christmas: one thing they need, one thing to play with, and one thing to read.
- Children receive only four gifts for Christmas: something they want, something they need, something to wear, and something to read.
- Children receive only four gifts for Christmas: something huggable, something musical, something readable, and something never advertised on TV.
- Children receive one nice gift each.
- Decide to forgo gift giving among family members. Instead, use the money to take a trip together. For example, you could visit one of the various Church history sites.
- Agree to buy gifts only for the children in the extended family, not parents or teens.
- Draw names for gifts among family members (immediate or extended) to simplify how many gifts you have to give. If you don't want to draw names, you can rotate gift assignments.
- Instead of giving gifts to each other, donate the money you would have spent to a charity or community food pantry (see chapter 9 for more ideas).
- Instead of buying gifts, each family member makes a present for another family member using only supplies that are around the house. Rotate names each year.
- Establish a family rule that all family gifts must be given from the heart, but they have to make it, bake it, sew it, or grow it.

- Instead of expensive presents, give only stockings to family members. Children fill parents' or grandparents' stockings. Draw names from all family members so that everyone has one stocking to fill. This works out well when all of your children are older.
- Instead of receiving stockings on Christmas morning, use them to spread the giving out. Put something small in your children's stocking every day of the week prior to Christmas, for the twelve days before Christmas, or the twelve days between Christmas and Epiphany (this is called Christmastide).
- For the twelve days of Christmas, siblings fill each other's stockings with small surprises or coupons. Then, after family prayer, children retrieve their stocking to see what the day has brought.
- Instead of giving children stockings on Christmas morning, give them on another designated giving day, such as St. Lucia's. Use the customs of the countries from which your ancestors came.
- Siblings pool their resources together and get one big gift for Mom and Dad.
- Set limits on children's want lists. For instance, they can only ask for a prearranged amount of gifts, such as two toys and one article of clothing.
- Have children collect some of their toys in good condition. Clean and wash them to donate to the ward nursery or to a shelter. Some families require their children to do this before Santa can leave any new toys, while some families have children leave one nice toy of theirs under the tree for Santa to give to another child.
- Set a limit on the dollar amount to spend on each gift, such as five or ten dollars. Gifts can be purchased at thrift stores, yard sales, or craft stores. This can be a fun challenge to see what type of gifts family members come up with.
- Challenge children to spend no more than one dollar for their friends, or to limit their gift giving to a few close friends.
- Mom takes children to a dollar store to give them an opportunity to shop for an inexpensive present for Dad, and then supervises the wrapping. On another day, Dad takes children to the

dollar store to shop for Mom. Or, Mom helps children make a present for Dad, and then Dad helps children make a present for Mom.
- Children draw names of siblings out of a hat. With a set dollar amount, parents take them, one at a time, out for lunch and some one-on-one time so the child can pick out a present for the sibling.
- Create a "mommy store." Buy a few small toys appropriate for children in the family. Then children earn tokens by doing extra chores around the house that they can spend at the mommy store to buy gifts for their brothers and sisters.
- Give "time gifts" to someone else in the family by allocating blocks of time during the holiday to spend just with them.
- Give coupons as a way to give the gift of time. These can be as simple or elaborate as you choose, and can be for service that you perform for the recipient, or time spent doing an activity with them. (If you give someone a coupon book, insist that the coupons be redeemed. If they aren't, it will be as if you never gave a present. Suggest a time you will get back to them if they have not redeemed their coupon. And if you receive a coupon, be sure to redeem it.)
- Give children reverse coupons that can be used to excuse them from doing their chores for the day.
- Instead of giving grandchildren gifts, give them the present of your presence. Take them out individually for an activity, or go shopping with them and allow them to choose a small gift that they would enjoy. Designate a dollar amount that they can spend.
- Grandma and Grandpa buy each other presents, but presents have to be an item that can be played or shared with the grandchildren when they come to visit, such as a game or toy.
- Grandparents purchase new church clothes for the grandchildren to remind them of the importance of worshipping the Savior year round.

MAKE GIFT GIVING A FUN EVENT

Give children the responsibility of making Christmas fun by creating ways to extend or replace giving so that the focus is on the process and not on the present.

- Have a gift exchange game. Everyone brings one gift worth a certain dollar amount. Pick numbers from a bowl, and the person who draws number one gets the first choice of gift. Number two gets to choose from the pile or the gift that number one took. Number three picks from the pile or the number one or number two gifts, until all the gifts are distributed. You can open the presents before the next one decides, or open all the gifts when everyone has chosen one.
- Using a variation of the gift exchange game, number all the presents as they are received. Then pick numbers from the bowl, and the number that you pick is the number of gift that you receive. Open the gifts one by one.
- Instead of putting names on the presents under the tree, number them. At dinner on Christmas Eve, everyone receives a candy bar for dessert with a number on it. These numbers can be matched with the numbers on the gifts.
- Organize a Christmas gift treasure hunt. Come up with clues for each of the children's gifts (they could be in rhyme, if you are so inclined). The first clue is hidden somewhere in the Christmas tree, which leads to a gift stashed somewhere else in the house, along with another clue to the next.
- Begin a gag gift tradition. Exchange only presents that are silly and within a specified dollar amount, or recycle a white elephant back and forth by coming up with a crazy way of getting it to the other person, such as delivering it by a pizza man, burying it inside another gift, and so on. This could be a fun way to get creative with extended family members, infuse some humor into family get-togethers, and help create good memories. (I remember fondly a white elephant exchange that took place at a party with some dear friends. One of the couples in our group brought a pair of worn garden shoes as a present, which was funny enough. But when someone opened them, another woman in the group saw them and exclaimed, "Wait! Those are *my* shoes!" She said she left them on the front step that past summer and couldn't figure out where they could have possibly gone. It's great when we can enjoy one another's company and have a good laugh at the same time!)
- Plan a "Twelve Days of Christmas" activity for a friend or

neighbor. Leave an anonymous gift for each of the twelve days of Christmas. These gifts can be large or small, or a combination of each, but it is nice to include some spiritual elements.

- Between family members or between friends, use the same Christmas jar or fancy tin to exchange homemade goodies back and forth.
- Start the tradition of passing the same Christmas gift box between family members. Each time a gift is given, the dates and names of the giver and receiver are recorded on the side of the box.

GIFTS FROM THE HEART

- Instead of giving gifts to brothers and sisters, consider writing a family history. Every year, all family members write an essay on a given topic, such as memories of past Christmases, positions held in the Church, happiest moments of their childhood, and so on. The topic could be assigned early in the year. These are collected and copied for everyone and given as a gift. On Christmas morning, enjoy reading wonderful memories.
- As a gift to parents or grandparents, present a binder where children all write five to ten things on several topics, such as "The Moment I Knew My Mother Loved Me," "The Most Surprising Thing I Ever Saw My Father Do," "The Kindest Thing I Have Seen My Mother Do," "My Father's Strongest Trait," or "Advice and Lessons My Parents Have Taught Me."
- Create a family history or journal with the stories of past Christmases. Parents, grandparents, and children could write memories of their favorite Christmas activities and the fun they had doing things together as a family. (My mother knew I would appreciate such a gift, so she wrote down her memories of her past Christmases, and it was delightfully received.)
- Buy a journal or notebook for each family member and write a tribute to them on the first page.
- Compose a "Top 10 List of Things I Remember About My Dad (or Mom)," along with entries from other siblings.
- Create a photo album or scrapbook during the year when more time is available.
- Write your personal history and give it as a cherished gift to your children.

- Interview family members about special things they remember about Grandma or Grandpa. Put these comments together with some family photos into a scrapbook for a cherished gift.
- Videotape an interview of your parents or grandparents about childhood memories—what it was like when they were young, how they met each other, what their Christmas traditions were, and so on. It's helpful if you have a list of questions to discuss, and it might be helpful if you gave a copy to them beforehand so they have time to think about their answers.
- Record the personal history of a grandparent or great-grandparent, using audiotape or videotape. Type the written stories to be given to extended family members and all future descendants. (My younger sister spent hours transcribing my grandfather's audiotapes of his life and stories. It was truly a gift from the heart and one that I received with pleasure and gratitude.)
- Videotape or audiotape yourself sharing your testimony of the Savior for grandchildren to have in years to come.
- Videotape grandchildren doing different activities during the season, such as baking cookies, trimming the tree, or playing in the snow, and send the video to grandparents who can't be there for Christmas.
- Videotape your young child telling his or her account of the Christmas story. Have the child draw a picture to accompany the story. Grandma and Grandpa will love receiving this as a gift.
- Copy and frame old family photographs, or give new photographs.
- Compile a collection of favorite holiday stories that can be read each day before Christmas and give to neighbors as a gift.
- Create a unique CD slide show presentation using an uplifting and spiritual theme. (Lorie, a close friend of mine, put together a CD with a slide show presentation of beautiful pictures of the Savior put to reverent songs and carols and gave them as gifts. They were inspiring.)
- Prepare a CD photo slide show for family members to watch and enjoy. (My good friend Jan, who has several married children, tells me that every year her children take turns

collecting photos of the whole family for the past year. Then at their family Christmas party, they watch the photo slide show of everyone's pictures. Copies on discs are given to everyone as a gift, and it has become a favorite and cherished family tradition.)

- Write a letter to a family member, telling him or her how much you appreciate them and the things they do for you. Wrap it and put it under the tree.
- Make it a tradition to write a letter to each child, expressing love and appreciation for them, and then save their Christmas letters in a scrapbook or binder for them.
- Every year, husbands and wives write a love letter to each other detailing their appreciation and love for having the privilege of being together for another year.
- Instead of purchasing gifts for each other, each spouse comes up with ideas for six dates for the coming year, thus giving the couple one special date a month. Present them as illustrated gift certificates or in other creative ways. (I'm indebted to my close friend Barb, who shared with me this beautiful tradition that she and her husband began a couple of years ago. They were so creative in coming up with unique and wonderful dates, and I can't wait to try this one!)
- Give your spouse twelve coupons, each redeemable for a temple session and a treat or dinner afterward.
- Give the gift of time. Think about ways you could help family, friends, or neighbors by taking their children for an hour or two so that parents can have a little time to catch their breath, finish shopping, or whatever they might need.
- Send a friend a postcard telling about a gift you plan to give him or her. For instance: "I'll pick your child up at 10:30 AM on December 15 for lunch and a movie so you can get some shopping done."
- Using a small token such as a star or an angel, family members perform acts of service for each other during the month, leaving the token there to be passed on to someone else when a kindness is performed.
- For family home evening each week between Thanksgiving and Christmas (or you can start as early as the first Monday in

November), draw names to give one another gifts of kindness, service, or good deeds. This way, family members get a chance to serve different people.
- Create a "secret angel" tradition. Draw names from a hat, and then be a secret angel for that person for the rest of the holiday season. Two important rules: no gift buying and absolute secrecy. The secret angel, for instance, could make the other child's bed, do one of his chores, or leave a note or another token of appreciation for the person. This is a great way to teach children that what they do is often the most appreciated gift of all.
- Compliment at least three people every day in December. This is a gift that is always appreciated.
- Pick someone on your holiday card list or a friend that you haven't talked to for some time, and strengthen your friendship by calling or writing a long letter to the person.
- Give a gift to someone who is not expecting one. You could say that you are not trying to start a habit of exchanging gifts, but you are grateful for their friendship.
- Make a gift cookbook of cherished family recipes and give it to other family members. Or give a copy of easy-to-cook recipes to newly married children or to missionaries. (Last year, my sister put together a cookbook of their family's cherished recipes and gave it to all her children. It was a delightful gift, and I was greatly honored that she would give me a copy.)
- Write a poem for a loved one and prepare a creative way to present it.
- Draw or sketch a picture to give to a loved one.
- Make a CD mix of your spouse's favorite music and give it to him to listen to.
- Make a recording of your musical talents and give it to your family. (One year my mother gave me a CD of her playing her favorite songs on the piano. It was a wonderful gift!)
- Make a tape of your family singing Christmas hymns and send it to extended family members.
- Record a grandfather or grandmother reading a favorite Christmas book. Send it to a grandchild along with the book and a small cuddly blanket to cuddle and to remember grandparents who can't be there.

- Give family keepsakes, such as antique jewelry or trinkets, to family members.
- Make a family picture calendar and mark important dates and birthdays, along with recent family photos. These can be easily made at copy stores.
- Have a cherished photo laminated on a tote bag. Photo transfer paper from the craft store that can be used on almost anything.
- Make an apron (or buy one) and using fabric paint, decorate the apron with handprints from all the grandchildren to give to grandmother.

GIVE A GIFT TO CHRIST

President Faust said, "Anciently the three wise men came from afar to bring gifts to the baby Jesus. Would it not be marvelous this Christmas if we could personally give gifts to the Savior? I believe this is possible to do."[3] The following are a few ideas of ways to give to the Savior. For more ideas on service-oriented gifts, see chapter 9.

- Send copies of the Book of Mormon with your testimony written inside to missionaries serving from your ward. Or give a copy to a friend or neighbor.
- Invite a nonmember friend to attend the First Presidency Christmas Devotional broadcast with you. You may also choose to invite less active members to a sacrament meeting in December or to your ward Christmas party.
- Give gifts to a stranger, an enemy, someone in need, and to Christ. Take someone who is hungry out to dinner or deliver food to a family in need; invite a stranger to spend part of your holiday with you; send small gifts and cards to a nearby prison; visit a pediatric hospital or a nursing home.
- Take the opportunity to bear your testimony whenever you can during the Christmas season—in a ward meeting, to a friend, to family member, or to a stranger.
- Donate to the missionary fund.
- Resolve to smile at everyone you meet, or be the first person to say hello. Go out of your way to be kind and helpful and to spread Christmas cheer.
- Give the gift of gratitude. Send a thank-you card or handwritten note to someone you appreciate. (I knew a sweet elderly lady

who would send me a thank-you card every time I gave a Relief Society lesson, visited her, or stopped to chat with her in the store. Inez Bergeson had more grace in her little finger than I will ever have in a lifetime, and her notes were sweet, sincere, and very appreciated.)

- Make an entry in your journal thanking the Lord for all the gifts He has given. Write about what you would like to give Him for Christmas and how you will try to make Christmas more meaningful.
- Take a treat to someone who has been special to your family during the year. Give him an anonymous note explaining what he has meant to you. Deliver it to a doorstep, ring the doorbell, and run. Or phone afterward and let him know that someone has left him a gift.
- Give a tangible gift to the Savior by giving new copies of hymn books to the ward, donating a new book to the ward library, or purchasing a new toy for the nursery.
- Take time to thank store clerks while shopping. You'll probably make their day.
- Make a "Gift of Love" tree. This could be made of green felt and hung on the wall, with a pocket for each member of the family. Or it could be a little evergreen tree with envelopes tied to the branches with ribbons. These gifts of love are notes of appreciation, love, and thanks to family members, and are placed on the tree during the season and read on Christmas Eve.
- Work on your genealogy during December and find at least one name to turn in for the temple work to be done.
- Devote the Christmas season to giving as Christ gives, to forgiving as Christ forgives, and to loving others as Christ loves us.

FAMILY GIFTS TO THE SAVIOR

My neighbor Lori shared with me the story of when her four-year-old brother came home from Primary one day shortly before Christmas and began to rummage anxiously through the presents under the tree. After not finding what he was searching for, he became upset and explained that his Primary teacher had told him that Christmas was Jesus' birthday, yet there were no presents under the tree for Him. Where were the presents for Jesus? In response, their family developed the tradition of wrapping a box and placing it as the first present under their tree. The box would have a slit in the top where small slips of paper could be placed following each kind deed performed. On Christmas Day, the box was unwrapped and the deeds were shared with the family. A visual reminder of everyday acts of kindness can help to cultivate the Spirit and to remind children of the importance of giving back to the Savior. The following are several different ways that this may be done:

- In Brazil, they have a tradition of beginning the season by giving the Savior a "white gift." Every year, members of the community wrap items of food in white paper and take these gifts to the Nativity in the center of the town. These gifts in turn are given to the poor and the hungry during the coming month. Leaving a box under the tree or on the mantle for a collection of kind deeds is very similar to this, and the box could be wrapped in white paper with a picture of the Savior on it. Your family could then open the present to Jesus on Christmas Eve during a family fireside.
- Prepare a stocking for Jesus. It should be different from your family's stockings, perhaps made of white satin. Place slips of paper inside indicating what you intend to give the Savior during the coming year, such as reading the Book of Mormon before next Christmas, mending a relationship with a family member, or another self-improvement gift from the heart. These could be placed in envelopes with the giver's name on them, and they could be opened privately the following Christmas Eve. Waiting until Easter would give added symbolism to the gift that Jesus was born for us, and more important, that He died for us and was resurrected. It would also help children understand that acts of kindness are important all year long, not just during December.
- On the Monday before Christmas, have a family home evening where you talk about the gifts you want to give to the Savior. Write down the gift on a piece of paper and place it in a small box, such as a jewelry box. Wrap each family member's box and put the gifts around a wooden manger. On Christmas Eve, open the gifts and talk about them.
- Many families have the familiar custom of building a manger and filling it with straw, one piece at a time, for each good deed

rendered. Hopefully, by Christmas, the baby Jesus has a soft bed to lie on.
- Use a nicely decorated box as a good deed box. Drop in notes throughout the season that describe the surprises that others have prepared for us or other Christlike service that we observe from people around us. Put in all kindnesses, large or small. Open the box on Christmas Eve and read the accounts.
- Fast on Christmas Eve to renew your testimony of the Savior. Fasting heightens all your senses. Taste, sights, and sounds seem more vivid, and the spiritual feelings become more sacred.
- Some families hold a cottage meeting for nonmembers at a family home evening during the holidays. They sometimes also carol to a nonmember family and then invite them to their home for the evening.
- Give the gift of gratitude. As you hang each ornament on your tree, name something that the Lord has blessed you with or something that you are thankful for.
- Create a family gratitude journal. Pass the book around at family gatherings and allow everyone who is in attendance to add an entry in the family keepsake.
- During Christmas dinner, everyone takes a turn expressing gratitude for something that has meant a lot to them during the past year.
- After opening your presents, hug all your family members and tell them they are the best gift of all.

CHAPTER 7

give all year

One of the things I like so much about Christmas is that it opens people's hearts, and we tend to be a little kinder and a little more friendly. The world seems more open to charitable giving and reaching out to those in need. This is the time of the year that "if there is anything virtuous, lovely, or of good report or praiseworthy, we seek after these things" (Articles of Faith 1:13). We begin to act more like the Latter-day Saints we ought to be.

As Saints and disciples of Jesus Christ, we endeavor to walk in the footsteps of the Savior. Sometimes, however, we stumble and fall under the heavy load, particularly if we are only accustomed to wearing the sandals of discipleship once a year. We should not wait until Christmas to start seeking Christ, or we may find out too late that our sandals need a little breaking in.

Like little children toddling after a loving parent, we need to keep our eyes on the Savior so that we will not lose sight of Him. The closer we are to Him, the easier it will be to walk in His footsteps each and every day.

To the disciples and followers of Christ, each day is a new opportunity to keep His commandments. Every day we should strive to serve and love others and live our lives in accordance with His teachings. Instead, we often try to crowd a whole year of kindness and charity into one short month. But I don't think when He taught us to serve others He had in mind random bursts of enthusiasm followed by long periods of silence. His sheep need to be fed each day.

DON'T WAIT UNTIL CHRISTMAS

Love is not limited to a week or a day each year. God loves all his children every day of the year, and parents do not ration their appreciation for their families. I believe that a gift received in June—especially if given sincerely and received unexpectedly—is as welcome as one given in December. There is no need to wait for the Christmas season to be charitable or to be our best.

Sister Richards, in answering the question that I referred to earlier about how a Mormon Christmas should be different, also explained,

> Is the unloading of gifts and toys on those who really don't need them in keeping with the Spirit of Christ? Think of all the unhappy children who see other children loaded down with gifts when, due to circumstances they often cannot understand, they receive very little. Think of unhappy parents who go into debt or do without necessities while trying to keep up with the neighbors. Think of the selfishness these things cause and the false values they create.
>
> The clothes and other practical gifts so often given can be spread along the way. Given when most needed, they bring a lot of surprise and joy throughout the year. Even toys would bring more happiness and make many days special if they were given for several occasions rather than all at once.[1]

Sister Richards's comments validated my feelings and gave me the courage to go against what I viewed as common protocol. I could give presents whenever I wanted to. I didn't have to put so much emphasis on giving to my children at Christmastime. I could spread it throughout the year. I loved the advice, and it sounded very reasonable. Her philosophy just seemed to be an extension of our previous decision to simplify Christmas.

USE THE ELEMENT OF SURPRISE

In the first year that we first started our three gifts tradition, I had already made some stuffed Pound Puppies for all my children, but I didn't want to give them all the same thing to cherish. I decided to try this approach and put them away to use as a surprise at a later day. Then, on one cold late January morning, the children awoke to a new friend staring them in the face. The squeals of delight were awesome! We had never seen this kind of reaction from a Christmas morning present. Those puppies were literally loved to pieces. It was so much fun to surprise our children in this way, and I was hooked.

In exchange for cutting back on Christmas gifts, we would give more throughout the year, but mostly at unexpected times. I didn't know what a fun tradition it would become for me to give a wrapped present whenever I felt like someone needed a little extra boost, and it was always very well received. Telling a child you are thinking of him or that you are proud of him is so satisfying to both parent and child. If I saw something on sale, I would buy it and put it away for just the perfect moment.

It was fun to give gifts on other holidays when gifts were unexpected. But in order to keep the element of surprise, we tried not to be consistent, which is somewhat opposite of most traditions. In reality, the tradition wasn't to receive gifts but for us as parents to show our love for them by giving them pleasant surprises and affirmations.

We have given gifts for Groundhog's Day, the Fourth of July, the first day of school, and the last day of school, to name a few. The only consistent times we have given gifts has been for birthdays and Halloween. Because our children had food allergies, they couldn't eat most of the candy they would receive from trick-or-treating. So in exchange for all their candy, we would offer them a nice wrapped surprise. It was always a fair trade, and they didn't seem to feel too deprived.

My favorite surprise, though, was given during a family home evening that we had just before Valentine's Day with all of our grown children and their families. We discussed that families are forever. Although it was a concept we had often talked about, it took on extra meaning when we used unexpected, carefully chosen gifts to illustrate that we want to give good gifts to our children. We likened it to our Father in Heaven, who also wants to give us gifts and has given us the best gift of all—the chance for families to be together forever.

Unexpected surprises gave us many opportune moments to teach, but we also discovered that gifts may be used as motivational tools. I remember fondly the October day when I placed two wrapped presents on top of the fridge where the kids could see them. When my sons, ages eleven and nine, saw the presents, they were naturally curious about them. I explained that the presents were rewards for anyone who helped clean out the garden for winter. It was a big task, and I didn't think they were up for the challenge. But much to my delight, those boys were outside at 8:00 the next morning, in cold and rainy weather, for several hours. They did a fantastic job, and they more than deserved the reward that they proudly accepted.

HOW WE FOSTER GREEDINESS

President Faust reminds us of the importance of overcoming greed: "The message of this season that is applicable throughout the year lies not in the receiving of earthly presents and treasures but in the forsaking of selfishness and greed and in going forward, seeking and enjoying the gifts of the Spirit."[2]

Greed is fueled by the anticipation and the expectation of material goods, not just by children but by adults as well. Imagine, for instance, that you have just won $10,000. How long would it take you before you began to think about the things you planned to spend it on? If you were not accustomed to having much, the money would probably be used for necessities, such as food, clothing, or bills. A long list of wants would probably not be entertained because you would just be grateful for the pleasant surprise. However, if all of your financial needs had already been met, your list of wants could grow rapidly. Somewhere between needs and wants is where greed begins to grow.

That's the problem with Christmas. As children anticipate the presents they may receive, everyone around them fuels their anticipation by stressing the excitement and thrill of Christmas morning. Parents do it, teachers do it, friends and playmates do it as they ask, "What do you want for Christmas?" The children's imaginations can't help but conjure up all kinds of thoughts about all the wonderful toys they have ever seen.

Children whose basic needs have not always been met imagine a new coat or a simple doll or toy truck. Life has taught them that they can be happy with even the smallest surprises. But imagination holds no bounds for those children who have already been taught to expect the excesses of life. Greed begins to set in, and the children who already have more are the ones who unfortunately want more and more. It's no wonder their parents feel they have to step it up and buy more so that they don't shatter their children's expectations.

The best way to stop inadvertently teaching children to be greedy is to set clear and concise limits. Purposefully placed, they remind children that they can be happy with less. This way, imagination and expectation don't have much of a chance to expand their needs into unmet expectations. This is a huge benefit of giving the three wise gifts. Parents and children alike know exactly what to expect. That is wise indeed.

During the year, when they least expect it or anticipate it, children can then be given more of the things that parents really want to give them and for the right reasons. Children will not have unmet expectations, and parents won't feel resentment. I believe that gifts will not cause greed if given as a surprise and in moderation. A gift is far more valuable to a child who isn't expecting it. However, if the gifts become excessive, expectation comes back into play and all the benefits will dissipate.

AVOID THE JANUARY HUM-DRUMS

Too often we become so involved in our Christmas preparations that as soon as the day is over, the tree comes down—both literally and figuratively. We have grown weary of the hurried pace, and we want to get back to our normal routines. So we pack away the ornaments and the garlands, and we heave a huge sigh of relief because Christmas is over.

As the Christmas season winds down, we move into the January hum-drums. Many experience bouts of winter depression, and the month seems to go on forever. If we find ourselves feeling this way, we should remember the analogy of the spoon. If you hold a spoon with the bowl facing you, your image is displayed upside down and distorted. It is only when the spoon is turned outward that the image of one's self becomes right again.

We often feel let down in January because our focus shifts from outward to inward. We will not have the correct perspective in our own lives until we turn our view outward to others. However, the only way we can do this is if we do not empty our physical, emotional, and spiritual reserves during December.

CHRISTMAS IS A LIFESTYLE

We should celebrate Christmas a little bit at a time every day throughout the year. It should not be an event but rather a lifestyle. David Grayson, a famous writer of the nineteenth century, wrote, "I sometimes think we expect too much of Christmas Day. We try to crowd into it the long arrears of kindliness and humanity of the whole year. As for me, I like to take my Christmas a little at a time, all through the year. And thus I drift along into the holidays, let them overtake me unexpectedly, waking up some fine morning and suddenly saying to myself: 'Why, this is Christmas Day!' "[3]

An anonymous writer penned the following:

> So remember, while Christmas
> Brings the only Christmas Day—
> During the year let there be Christmas
> In the things you do and say.

We should give more spontaneously throughout the year—freely, without expecting anything in return. For most, this is a different way of looking at our past gift-giving behavior. As we do this, we will realize that the best gifts are not large or expensive. They can be as simple as acts of kindness given at opportune moments. When we have fostered the lifestyle of Christmas, we will become more observant of the needs of others, we will increase our capacity for charity, and our lives will begin to reflect our divine heritage as God's children.

After taking the first step to a meaningful Christmas by simplifying gift giving, I gained a conviction about the benefits of giving throughout the year. I had not imagined that Christmas would become so instrumental in teaching me how to love and serve others. People need my gifts throughout the year, just as we need the good gifts from the Savior not just for one day or one month, but every day and always. "The Work of Christmas," by Howard Thurman, reminds me that Christmas should be a year-round adventure:

> When the song of the angel is stilled,
> When the star in the sky is gone,
> When the kings and princes are home,
> When the shepherds are back with their flock,
> The work of Christmas begins:
> To find the lost,
> To heal the broken,
> To feed the hungry,
> To release the prisoner,

To rebuild the nations,
To bring peace among brothers,
To make music in the heart.[4]

Notes

1. Helen K. Richards, "What Should Be Different About a Mormon Christmas?"
2. James E. Faust, *The True Gifts of Christmas* (Salt Lake City: Eagle Gate Publishing, 2002), 13.
3. Ray Stannard Baker (pen name David Grayson). Works not copyrighted in the U.S.
4. Howard Thurman, "The Work of Christmas," *The Mood of Christmas and Other Celebrations* (Richmond: Friends United Press, 1973), 23.

CHAPTER 8

create meaningful family experiences

In Dr. Suess's book *The Grinch Who Stole Christmas*, the mean and nasty Grinch tries to stop Christmas from coming to the town of Who-ville, only to come to the following realization:

> He hadn't stopped Christmas from coming! It came!
> Somehow or other, it came just the same!
> And the Grinch, with his grinch-feet ice-cold in the snow,
> Stood puzzling and puzzling: "How *could* it be so?"
> "It came without ribbons! it came without tags!"
> "It came without packages, boxes or bags!"
> And he puzzled three hours, till his puzzler was sore.
> Then the Grinch thought of something he hadn't before!
> "Maybe Christmas," he thought, "*doesn't* come from a store.
> "Maybe Christmas . . . perhaps . . . means a little bit more!"[1]

We would be wise to come to this conclusion ourselves—that Christmas doesn't come from a store and it has little to do with presents. When we have simplified these distractions that can rob our family of the spirit of Christmas, we will then find more time to do the activities that create meaningful family memories. This will help us to make the deliberate shift away from the trap of materialism by strengthening our personal relationships.

CHRISTMAS IS ABOUT RELATIONSHIPS

Christmas is about light, warmth, and relationships. It's about spending time with people we love and doing things that enhance our time together. When that becomes the emphasis, we will experience more joy. The most memorable experiences that we will have at Christmas will be those that touch our hearts and enrich our spirit.

All of the traditions, activities, and events of Christmas are the modes of transportation along our journey, but they are not our final destination. Our destination is the strengthening of our bonds as an eternal family.

In an online article, Darla Isackson said the following, "Parents communicate the value and wonder of their children by giving time, by giving their presence, by giving themselves. It takes a clear vision of what matters to give our children presence, not just presents. We fill the errand . . . of angels only by our presence. We cheer and bless mainly by our presence—our willing presence. Our presence that is wholehearted, not fragmented by unreasonably hefty to-do lists."[2]

The Christmas season can be an ideal time for enlarging our children's empathy for others and for experiencing the true meaning of family togetherness. We can teach them by example that there are much more meaningful ways to have fun during the holiday besides opening presents.

CHRISTMAS IS ABOUT MEMORIES

When we remember the special times in our lives, we don't usually remember material things, but we remember the experiences we have had with family and friends. I have many wonderful memories of my childhood Christmases, but I don't remember most of the presents I received. Instead, my memories are filled with my parents' enthusiasm for Christmas and the fun that we had together as a family.

I remember how my dad loved Christmas and how much he loved decorating the tree. I remember how he taught us to carefully place the ornaments and the icicles in just the right spots. I also remember how he loved all kinds of Christmas music. One of my favorite childhood memories is of his reel-to-reel tape player. He recorded hours of every possible kind of Christmas music onto reels that would last the entire day, and then he rigged up speakers to the outside of the house so that he could play Christmas carols to anyone passing by. Making snow angels is fun, but doing it while listening to "Hark the Herald Angels Sing" is much more fun! It was even fun to shovel the walk as long as there was beautiful music playing. Maybe it was his way of getting us out of the house, but it worked!

Another memory of mine is the time when we were living on the coast of Cape Cod and were snowed in for a week with drifts of snow well over six feet deep. My dad dug a network of tunnels in the snow for us to run through, and we could go from the front door all the way to a large igloo at the end of the tunnel. I was only five years old, but I still remember it clearly.

Other fun memories included driving around in the car on Christmas Eve to look at the lights (probably to help us calm down!). Then the day after Christmas, the whole family would work on a jigsaw puzzle that was so large it took a week to finish.

I also remember my mother's great cooking and the traditional foods we ate every year—ham, sour cream marshmallow salad, yummy sugar cookies, and carrot pudding with warm white sauce. Those were simple days when we delighted in making ice cream from snow (at least we called it ice cream). Mom would put out pans to collect the freshly fallen snow and then whip it with sweetened condensed milk or evaporated milk and sugar. It had to be eaten quickly, but that was part of the fun.

I could go on with these memories of Christmases past, but I think these few examples illustrate how memories of good times spent together as a family become the legacy of our lives. These memories of the love we share together are the most important riches that we will ever possess, and we have the privilege of passing them down to our children.

We may not feel that these small, inconspicuous moments are very important in the eternal realm, but the Lord has told us, "Wherefore, be not weary in well-doing, for ye are laying the foundation of a great work. And out of small things proceedeth that which is great" (D&C 64:33).

CHRISTMAS IS ABOUT JOY

Many people say that Christmas is for children and is no longer meaningful when all the children have left home. When I hear this, I can't help but think about all the older couples I know who find creative and meaningful ways to be of service to those around them, and the joy that they receive from their Christmases. Many soul-enriching opportunities are available, so no one should feel deprived of memorable experiences, regardless of age, health, or marital status.

All we need is to open our hearts, our hands, and our eyes to look beyond ourselves. With a little creative imagination, we will find many opportunities to fill our hearts with Christmas spirit. There are concerts, plays, and wonderful public television presentations, to name a few. There are opportunities to strengthen our relationships with family and friends. There are so many chances to be of great worth in a volunteer position or to serve our neighbors. Being proactive in finding meaningful activities can make the difference between feeling sorry for ourselves or feeling joy with someone else.

The opportunities for us to love others and to feel love ourselves are all around us. Reaching out to others brings so much joy into our own lives. It just takes a little focus and determination to do those things that matter the most, to learn how to enjoy our families and friends more fully. This is a time to become playful, to enjoy a game with the children, or to just sit and cuddle and read a good Christmas book.

Experiencing meaningful activities together will help us achieve beautiful Christmas memories, kindling feelings of good will, appreciation, and even forgiveness. Our most memorable Christmases will be those when concerns and cares are pushed aside—as they should be—by the sight of Christmas lights and decorations, the sound of Christmas carols, the smell of pine and wassail, and feelings of being together with the ones we love.

If we are living in harmony with the Savior's teachings, peace and joy really can be ours. Hopefully we will find so much joy in serving the Lord and our family and enjoying one another's company that we will feel like Ammon, who said, "Therefore, let us glory, yea, we will glory in the Lord; yea, we will rejoice, for our joy is full" (Alma 26:16).

This chapter is dedicated to several ideas that promote family togetherness, many of which you may already do. One problem we often encounter is feeling tempted to try every possible activity that could bring our family closer together. However, if we cannot accomplish them in a leisurely and unrushed manner, we will be defeating our purpose in creating pockets of peace and moments of joy. It's better to have just a few really great experiences than to have twenty hurried ones. We don't need to feel the false urgency that taking on too many activities creates.

Notes
1. Dr. Seuss, *The Grinch Who Stole Christmas* (New York: Random House, 1985).
2. Darla Isackson, "Presence, Not Presents," *Meridian Magazine*, Dec. 20, 2007, http://www.meridianmagazine.com.

WAYS TO CREATE
meaningful
FAMILY EXPERIENCES

• ○ • ○ • ○ • ○ • ○ •

SHARE BEAUTIFUL MUSIC TOGETHER

Music is as important for Christmas now as it was for the angels on both sides of the veil who sang about the joyful events in Bethlehem. When my family watched the movie *The Nativity Story* and came to the part when angels rejoice, my grandson announced, "I think the loudest one was me!" What a beautiful thought! Everyone should have that kind of conviction about singing tidings of great joy.

Wouldn't it be wonderful if we could all remember witnessing Christ's birth, that sentinel moment in history when we rejoiced together in praise and in one accord! How grateful we must have been to witness that event—I doubt that any force in the universe could have kept us from singing those praises. Perhaps there are sparks of those memories still buried deep within that prompt us to want to sing when we think about the Savior—his birth, his life, his sacrifice, and his sublime gifts of the atonement and resurrection that allow us to live again.

Music has the ability to draw out memories that we have long ago forgotten. When memories surface, we once again recall the flood of feelings, convictions, and heart-felt emotions connected to our previous experiences. For this reason, it is important to safeguard this tool called music that has such a claim on our souls. Uplifting music, carols, and hymns that prompt positive and soul-enriching feelings are so important to our ability to experience the spirit of Christmas. Below are some ideas to help your family incorporate music into your Christmas celebrations. Below are some ideas to help your family incorporate music into you Christmas celebrations.

- Sing the songs of Christmas that reflect the Savior. Many people enjoy George Frederick Handel's *Messiah*, and often you may be able to find a local *Messiah* sing-in to participate in. Some people take time afterward to read the scriptures in Isaiah on which Handel based his oratorio.

- Listen to beautiful Christmas music. Music will fill your heart and home with a spirit of peace greater than any other activity. Choose songs that are reverent; minimize songs that have nothing to do with the real reason for the season. Look for new sources of beautiful music and even old Christmas songs that have been forgotten. Try something new or resurrect something old.
- Many families make a habit of attending a performance of *The Nutcracker* every year.
- Make it a custom to attend a concert of sacred Christmas music. Expose your family to as much beautiful Christmas music as possible. There are often free community concerts throughout the season featuring local singing groups.
- Purchase a new Christmas CD for your collection every year.
- Serenade your family with a new Christmas carol every day on the piano.
- Play Christmas carols together on homemade chimes made from metal pipes. Patterns for Christmas Music and Pipe Wind Chimes can be found at www.kidsactivitybox.com.
- Play carols on a CD player outside as children play in the snow.
- Write a Christmas song and share it with friends and neighbors as a gift, or sing it in your family night or Christmas Eve devotional.
- Invite another family over for a musical family night. Invite anyone who has musical talent to play an instrument or to sing a song. Anyone who is not musically inclined may choose to do a reading or a share a favorite Christmas story.
- Use your cultural heritage to have an enjoyable music experience. If your family is of German ancestry, teach your children how to sing "Silent Night" in German. Families of Scandinavian background often enjoy joining hands and circling around the Christmas tree while they sing their customary carols.
- Have a family devotional each evening during the month of December. Sing a different carol after discussing the meaning of the lyrics.

- Families who cannot get together for the holidays sometimes remember each other by singing a favorite song at an appointed time, such as holding hands at exactly 8 PM on Christmas Eve and singing "Silent Night."
- Caroling lifts the spirits of both those who sing and those who hear. Gather together friends and family to sing carols at a local nursing home or hospital, giving much needed comfort to the elderly or those who are ill.
- Invite other families to go caroling with your family in the neighborhood. You could leave a plate of cookies or another treat at each home, and perhaps even a copy of the Book of Mormon. Children could carry bells to ring as you walk from home to home. Carry taper candles placed in clear plastic disposable glasses (cut an X in the bottom of the cup to insert the candle). Upon returning home, serve hot chocolate or apple cider and Christmas cookies to those who participated.
- Go "car caroling" with your family. Roll down the windows, turn up the heat, and sing as loud as you can into the winter air as you slowly drive through the neighborhood.

READ CHRISTMAS STORIES TOGETHER

My favorite Christmas stories come from a book called *Christmas I Remember Best* published by the Deseret News Publishing Company in Salt Lake City, Utah. It was a compilation of stories from the newspaper (the tradition started in 1959). These stories were almost always tender and poignant, and if you can get your hands on a copy of this out-of-print book, by all means hang onto it!

- Read stories of inspiration each night in December. Good sources are the *New Era* and the *Ensign*—keep December issues and refer to them in years to come, or access them on www.lds.org. Follow your story with a family prayer. Other sources include books with collections of short stories from various authors, or booklets that can be purchased every year. Recently the *Church News* has included several stories from the lives of various general auxiliary leaders and General Authorities. And, there is no shortage of Christmas stories on the Internet, but be selective. Choose stories about giving,

sharing, and sacrificing, not about Rudolph or Santa.
- Many different newspapers publish inspirational stories between Thanksgiving and Christmas, and sometimes these real stories make for the best reading.
- Some families make it a custom to acquire a new Christmas book each year. There are many beautiful ones to choose from, and the choices range from children's stories to adult versions. Choose books that emphasize the reason for the season.
- Some people (including President Monson) make it a custom to read *The Christmas Carol* every year.
- Read from *Jesus the Christ* by James Talmage every morning and from the scriptures every night.
- Take the time to read a Christmas book to your children every night during December. Avoid stories about Santa and reindeer. Some families make this into an advent reading adventure by wrapping twenty-five children's Christmas books that they have collected over time. Each evening a child gets to pick out a present and unwrap it, followed by reading time. If children are old enough, designate certain nights for them to be the readers. As an alternative to wrapping the books, write the title of each book on small pieces of paper that are then placed into a jar or Christmas container. Children then take turns picking the titles. This is a good option if you want to cut down on the amount of wrapped presents in your home.
- Snuggle up in a favorite Christmas quilt each night to read the story of the day and rotate whose bed you snuggle in.
- After dinner every night, put on nice Christmas music, light the candles and the tree, and sit on the floor in a big circle as one person takes a turn reading a story that imparts the true meaning of Christmas.
- Exchange meaningful Christmas books with siblings at Thanksgiving to enhance your Christmas season.
- Prepare twelve new Christmas stories or poems every year as a gift for immediate or extended family members to read during the season.
- Create your own Christmas book by placing treasured stories in a binder and reading one a day during December or for the twelve days prior to Christmas.

- Create a Christmas Eve book and add to it each year. Fill a binder with favorite stories, scriptures, art, and music, and then use it during your family devotional on Christmas Eve.
- Keep a scrapbook to record the many Christmas memories for your family. Every year add a section about the year's celebration and include photos of family activities, meaningful letters and cards, and some journaling about what fun traditions you tried that year (and even the inevitable flops). You might also keep a record of the people who shared the holiday with your family and the Christmas card or letter that you sent out.
- I keep several binders full of beautiful pictures of Christ, cards, advent activities, and stories that I want to keep. I prefer to include pictures that show family activities rather than pictures of the kids unwrapping presents, as I am trying to create memories of family togetherness rather than gift giving.
- Create a tradition of keeping a guest book for visitors to sign when they come to your home. They can even leave a message if they like. You may choose to use loose Christmas papers that could easily be added to your Christmas scrapbook. As the years pass, this becomes a cherished memory of family and friends.

WATCH CHRISTMAS PROGRAMS TOGETHER

Some families turn off the television for the month of December, but I think that there are some wonderful musical programs available as well as other offerings. We simply need to be selective. When I was young, I loved the animated Christmas specials. But as a parent, I think that TV and movies should enhance our basic family values. We also need to ask ourselves if we are using the TV as a babysitter because we are rushing around doing far too many tasks.

Although some movies are fun to watch, they don't do much to promote the real reason for the season. There are fun Christmas movies that don't really focus on the birth of the Savior, although they portray positive values such as giving and sharing and have good entertainment value. We need to judge carefully what goes into the eyes, ears, and hearts of our loved ones, especially at a time when the adversary is so eager to deceive us.

Be very selective about the type of movies and TV specials that consume the family's valuable time. Start checking your local newspaper after Thanksgiving for a detailed list of TV specials and movies. By scheduling time to watch these programs, it will be easier to ensure quality viewing.

- Check out videos from your meetinghouse library about the life of the Savior, or obtain them from a Church distribution center or online at www.ldscatalog.com. You could watch *Finding Faith in Jesus Christ: The Ministries and Miracles of Jesus Christ (2002)* or the short video clip *Luke II*, which is included in a beautiful presentation of twenty-two short videos shown on the New Testament Video Presentations.
- Make it a family tradition to celebrate the birthday of the Prophet Joseph Smith on December 23 by viewing films based on historical accounts of his life. These could include *Legacy, Praise to the Man, Emma: My Story, The Life and Teachings of Joseph Smith,* and *the Work and the Glory* series.
- Have a Scrooge night where the family watches several different versions of The Christmas Carol. Favorites include the version with George C. Scott (1984), with Patrick Stewart (1999), but the most often preferred version is the 1951 version with Alastair Sim. (My family's favorite version is by far *The Muppet Christmas Carol* [1992]. Christmas wouldn't be Christmas at the Wamsleys without watching this movie!)
- Watch animated Christmas stories that focus on proper Christmas values. There aren't very many, but watch for *The Little Drummer Boy* (1968), *The Fourth Wise Man* (1985), *The Small One* (1978), and *A Charlie Brown Christmas* (1965).
- Watch a Christmas movie that has good family entertainment value. Choose your favorite finger foods and snacks to munch on while enjoying a classic favorite. Or make it a ritual to watch them while wrapping presents. Some favorites include *It's a Wonderful Life* (1946), *The Bells of St. Mary's* (1945), *Miracle on 34th Street* (1947), *The Bishop's Wife* (1947), *Christmas in Connecticut* (1945), and *White Christmas* (1954).
- Make it a tradition to watch favorite Latter-day Saint movies. These include *Mr. Krueger's Christmas* (1980), *Nora's Christmas Gift* (1989), *Ben's Gift,* and *The Forgotten Carols* (2008). Although not technically a movie made for Christmas, viewing *The Testaments of One Fold and One Shepherd* (2000) should definitely become a family tradition.

- Watch quality family films that instill positive Christian values, such as *The Christmas Box* (1995), *The Christmas Shoes* (2006), *Christmas Miracle of Johnathan Toomy* (2007), *The Nativity Story* (2007), and *The Ultimate Gift* (2006).

EAT CHRISTMAS FARE TOGETHER

For most families, feasting has always been an integral part of Christmas. It wouldn't be Christmas without that cherished recipe handed down from generation to generation. Perhaps it is English pudding with warm sauce, fruitcake, Danish stollen, rice pudding, raisin-filled cookies, popcorn balls, or poppy seed cake. Maybe it's the traditional turkey dinner or a honey-baked ham. Hot chocolate, wassail, eggnog, and cider seem to be the preferred beverages of the season.

Even if it is only eating finger sandwiches while watching Christmas movies, food plays a very important role in the gathering of families and even in gift giving. Our son Adam used to give his father chocolate covered cherries every year, and our daughter Sheena gives her dad the must-have mustard of the season with summer sausage. These are fun memories, but I must say that the most cherished ones are of the Christmas morning brunch Jay cooks the whole family every year.

- Combine forces with grown children to have a baking day. Rotate homes every year, and assign each person to bring a portion of the supplies after making the decision about which recipes to use. The hostess prepares a simple lunch and snacks. When finished for the day, divide up the goodies.
- Have an old-fashioned taffy pulling party.
- Mix a large bowl of gingerbread dough. Many families enjoy making gingerbread houses and gingerbread trains, not to mention gingerbread cookies. Making fragrant gingerbread boys and girls to hang on an old-fashioned tree is also a family favorite.
- Wrap mini gingerbread men with plastic wrap in a row with a ribbon between. Cut with scissors to give to friends when they visit, or use as an advent calendar and cut one off every day.
- Consider serving the same kind of food each year as you decorate the tree or deck the halls. Family members could bring appetizers or just order pizza. You may want to have cookies and hot chocolate, eggnog, or hot cider and homemade donuts. Whatever foods you choose, just enjoy the time spent together.

- Bake sugar cookies and have your children help decorate them. Place cookies in little baggies, tie with a ribbon, and put into a basket by the door to give to anyone who comes to visit.
- Have a baking party. Invite several people and assign each to bring one ingredient sufficient to make a large batch of cookies. Prepare the cookies together, and then deliver them to a homeless shelter or to other groups in need.
- Help your children bake Christmas breads or cookies to give to teachers, coaches, and school bus drivers.
- Make cookies that have a Christ-centered theme by telling your children the Christmas story as you cut out the different shapes. Use them to decorate your Christmas tree.
- Give out small plates of star-shaped cookies and attach a little card about the significance of the star of Bethlehem and Jesus, or use any other symbol, such as a candle, with a scriptural message about Christ.
- Let Mom have a break from the kitchen while the children bake some of the cookies and Mom takes some time to be by herself.
- Throw a fondue holiday party. Invite friends and family members, asking each person to bring a different food to dip. This could be a dessert fondue (such as chocolate or caramel) or a dinner fondue (cheese or meat cooked in oil). Many families have fondue for Christmas Eve dinner.
- Some families like to simplify dinner preparations at Christmastime. Some make lasagna ahead of time and freeze it, others have a Crock-Pot dinner, and others have a tradition of eating chili in purchased bread soup bowls.
- Many families prepare traditional cultural foods that have been handed down from generation to generation. Some have large Mexican dinners with homemade tamales and enchiladas for Christmas Eve. Others have a traditional seven-course Italian dinner, and still others have Slavic, Scandinavian, or German traditional foods. Research ethnic foods and prepare meals from the culture of your family's ancestors.
- Have a cookie exchange. Invite six friends to each bring seven dozen homemade cookies in packages of one dozen, along with six copies of the recipe. One dozen will be for eating, the rest for exchanging. The hostess also bakes seven dozen. Use one dozen

cookies from each person for serving with cider or eggnog. (Those not eaten can be taken to someone in need of kindness.) Everyone votes by secret ballot for the best, with the winner getting a simple prize. Everyone takes home six dozen cookies (but not of the kind they brought) and six new recipes.
- Have a candy exchange. This works in the same way as the cookie exchange, except that everyone makes candy instead of cookies.
- Plan a progressive dinner to have with friends during the season. A different course is held in each home, along with a spiritual message or story, and perhaps a small gift.
- Invite neighbors and friends to a dessert evening. Have everyone bring a different dessert to share, as well as a Christmas story. You could also consider asking the missionaries to participate.

DECORATE THE HOME TOGETHER

Decorate simply and modestly. Remember, anything that takes excessive time and energy may become a burden instead of a blessing (see chapter 5 for further discussion about simplifying decorating).

- When decorating for Christmas, use Christ-centered decorations that focus on the true meaning of the season, such as angels, candles, stars, Mary and Joseph, the wise men, shepherds, sheep, nativities, and so forth. Strive to stay away from decorations such as Santa, elves, and reindeer. Nutcrackers can be symbols of selflessness (see chapter 10).
- Delegate family members to decorate certain areas of the home—even young children are able to do some things. Take a picture of the area after it has been nicely decorated, and then keep all decorations for that area together in a box with the picture.
- Allow children to decorate their own tree with their favorite ornaments. This could be a smaller version of the family tree or a miniature in their bedrooms. If a miniature tree is used, it could be used as an advent tree with 25 ornaments for every day of December. If desired, attach to each ornament a note of appreciation and love.
- Children find a lot of delight in decorating their own rooms. They could put lights up around their windows, plastic clings on the windowpanes, and so on. Give each child a Nativity

scene of their own to keep in their bedroom. These don't have to be big or expensive; a small set will work just fine to remind them of the first Christmas.

- Collect Nativity scenes for the home instead of collections of Santa.
- Invest in a Nativity set that young children can play with. These can be made of plastic or resin for durability to withstand a lot of playtime.
- Have a "Deck the Halls" party. Set aside the same day every year, usually a Saturday, when the entire family decorates the house. Hang garlands, lights, wreaths, and stockings. Play carols on the stereo while you work.
- Have a tree-decorating party. Get the whole family together and make the activity fun. Parents who can no longer decorate their tree for themselves will especially enjoy this activity.
- Make luminaries to light the sidewalk, driveway, or outside stairs. Fill the bottom of a large lunch sack with at least one inch of sand. Fold the top of the bag back to keep it open. If desired, use an eyelet setter or awl to make holes in the sides of the paper sack and form pictures. Place a votive candle in the sand and light it for get-togethers or for Christmas Eve. Tradition says that luminaries lit the pathway for the Christ child, and historically they were used to guide people to Christmas mass.
- Make it a tradition to decorate a loved one's grave every year. Decorations might include a silk poinsettia or a Christmas wreath. On Christmas Eve, light candles or luminaries and place them on the grave. Have a graveside candlelight ceremony with a few carols and a prayer.
- When selecting or cutting down your Christmas tree, get an extra one to give to Grandpa and Grandma, an elderly neighbor, or a single mother.
- Keep pictures of the Savior and reminders of Him around the house in places where you are most likely to see them.

SPEND QUIET TIME TOGETHER

Take time together not only as a family but also as a couple. Remember that the most important thing we can give each other is our love, time, example, and precious memories.

- Choose a silent night to spend together as a couple or family. Turn off the TV, play soft music, and sit by the fire with hot chocolate. Savor the moment, and reflect on the joy of the season and the pleasure of being together. Or pop some corn and snuggle up with your favorite Christmas book or collection of stories.
- Take the family on an evening drive as often as you can to look at Christmas lights and to enjoy being together and listening to Christmas music. Pop some corn, and take the kids in their pajamas to help calm them and settle them down for sleep. Another option is to make this a surprise. Wait until the children are in bed, and then start making the popcorn. Scoop up the little ones and go light hunting.
- If you are in the vicinity, take the time to visit Temple Square in Salt Lake City. If not, go to see the light display at another temple. Or you may have a favorite drive-through display of lights that you like to visit, or perhaps an annual Christmas tree lighting.
- Write a thank-you note to someone who displays a Nativity scene in their front yard. Leave the note on their porch, perhaps with a small token gift. Or prepare a plate of cookies and hand deliver it with a personal word of thanks.
- Spiritually oriented coloring books are hard to come by. Sometimes you can find them at Christian bookstores. Or create your own by downloading various free illustrations and coloring pages from the Internet.
- Some families have a tradition where Mom and Dad go away for a night or a weekend to a bed and breakfast and spend some time relaxing and enjoying their time together as a couple.
- Arrange time to attend the temple to enhance your own spiritual experiences.
- Locate a live Nativity scene to visit. Sometimes these are listed in the newspaper, and may be presented by various denominations in your area, or sometimes by individual families. When children have the opportunity to view real people and real animals, they have an easier time visualizing the Nativity.
- Attend an international crèche display. These also are sometimes listed in the newspaper and may be sponsored by various

denominations. Collections of Nativity scenes from different countries are a wonderful reminder that people all around the world believe in the Savior, and it's a way for people of other faiths to understand that LDS members believe in Christ. The largest crèche display in the United States is the Midway Utah Stake Interfaith Crèche Display, which is held on the last Friday of November/first weekend in December. More than one thousand displays from countries all over the world fill almost every room, foyer, and hallway of the Midway Stake Center, and visitors come by the thousands over a four-day period.

- Another display, Crèches and Carols, is held in St. Louis, Missouri, and typically displays more than five hundred Nativity scenes. In the United States and Canada, at least fifty major Nativity exhibits take place every Christmas. With thousands of visitors each, an estimated 75 percent of these are hosted by wards and stakes of The Church of Jesus Christ of Latter-day Saints.
- Celebrate the birth of Joseph Smith on December 23. Invite family and friends for brunch or supper and read stories or watch videos about the prophet's life.
- If all your children are grown, choose a unique day other than Christmas where family members can celebrate with you. This way, they can then celebrate their own family traditions in their homes, and this gives you and your spouse more personal time for service and for spiritual reflection.
- Each evening, light several candles, one for each routine that children do before they hop into bed, such as reading the scriptures, brushing their teeth, and so forth. Blow out a candle after each routine is performed.

ADVENT TRADITIONS

Many religions celebrate different aspects of the Christmas season, beginning with Advent on the Sunday nearest to November 30 and progressing to Christmas Eve. Christmastide is celebrated the twelve days following Christmas and ends with Epiphany, or the arrival of the wise men, on January 6.

Advent is a Latin word meaning "the coming" and refers to four weeks set aside to contemplate not only the impending arrival of the birth of the Savior, but also the anticipation of His second coming. It was traditionally intended to be a time of personal introspection and growth by many churches, especially Catholics and Lutherans.

This season of advent progressed with the use of a calendar in the early 1900s that included small windows that could be opened to reveal pictures. These were helpful for young children anticipating the arrival of Christmas. Although the LDS Church does not celebrate the season of Advent as such, there are many traditions based on advent calendars to anticipate the arrival of Christmas.

- There are wonderful ideas for advent calendars that can be used during the season, but don't waste your time with the pictures of Santa and chocolate in the windows. Almost every year, the *Friend* magazine comes out with a new spiritual advent calendar, and these can be downloaded from www.lds.org. The *New Era* has also published spiritual advent calendars, or you can make your own.
- The simplest advent calendar to make is a chain made of paper strips, and many children make these at elementary school every year. Write activities or scriptures on the inside of the strips to help your children better feel the Christmas spirit.
- Read one scripture about the Savior each night as you burn a Christmas candle. Talk about the light and the love of the Savior, and commit to better follow in His light each day.
- A common advent calendar that is often used is a wall hanging with a felt tree. Twenty-four small pockets are attached to the bottom of the hanging, and they are large enough to hold small ornaments. Each day, an ornament is removed and hung on the tree. These ornaments could be symbolic, such as candles, bells, sheep, stars, and so on. Another option would be to attach a scripture that refers to the item and read it every day before the ornament is attached.
- For a more elaborate and spiritual calendar, create a quilted wall hanging with a stable. Every day, a different piece of the Nativity is hung on the calendar.
- Hang your stockings on December 1. Every day, children place in each other's stockings a small slip of paper with a compliment about each sibling, a note of thanks, or even an expression of love. Younger children can draw pictures. On Christmas Eve, the papers are read as the family bonds together in love.

- A scripture advent calendar is always a good idea for families. The calendar should contain pockets for scriptures relating to Christ's birth and life. Children can take turns removing the scriptures each day, and the family reads them together.
- Another idea for an advent activity is to use the twelve days before Christmas to discuss the Savior and his many gifts to us. Choose twelve topics, such as personal revelation, prayer, or prophets, and end with the gift of the Savior's birth. Each night the family discusses the significance of the gift.
- Gather or decorate twenty-four ornaments for a "service tree" and place them in a basket under the tree. Each time you complete an act of service, put an ornament on the tree. The family could choose which service to perform, or small slips of paper could be attached to each ornament that suggests an act of service.
- Use a service advent to count down to Christmas. Find a treat of some kind along with a scripture and an act of service to be performed that day, and wrap them nicely. Place the packages in a basket; when opened, the service must be performed in order to obtain the treat.
- Create a Christmas candle by placing twenty-five numbered marks along the side of a long candle. Each night, the family reads Christmas stories, sings carols, or reads scriptures until the candle burns down one number.
- Set up your manger scene on December 1, but place the wise men farther away since they have a long journey to Bethlehem. As Christmas approaches, place the wise men closer and closer to the manger. You may even want to wait to put the baby Jesus into the scene until you read the Christmas story on Christmas Eve.
- Using a replica of a wise man on a camel, start a tradition in which the wise man visits members of the family throughout the Christmas season to give them encouragement and spiritual advice. The wise man can be found every day throughout the season at a new location in the house as he continues on his journey to the Nativity scene. Sometimes he leaves messages, sometimes treats.

CHRISTMAS EVE TRADITIONS

- In honor of Jesus' birthday, bake a birthday cake and decorate it with white frosting. Place candles on the cake to symbolize that He is the light of the world. Children could help make and decorate the cake. Serve the cake on Christmas Eve or Christmas morning. Light the candles and sing "Happy Birthday."
- Have a birthday party for Jesus. Children bring a gift in honor of the baby such as canned foods, clothing, or toys. After celebrating with birthday cake, take the children to deliver their gifts to the appropriate place.
- Some families open all of their presents on Christmas Eve in order to make Christmas Day more spiritually oriented. Most people, however, prefer to keep Christmas Eve more sacred with a family spiritual devotional.
- Many families allow children to open one present just before bed, which is most often new pajamas so that the children will look nice in the morning when they have their pictures taken.
- On Christmas Eve, draw names of family members. You each have twenty-four hours to think of a service to give to that family member, which you will reveal on Christmas night.
- Have a formal Christmas Eve dinner. Set the table with your best china, goblets, and candles. Have everyone dress in Sunday best for this dinner and request that all family members use their best manners. Soft Christmas music can be played to set the mood for the Christmas devotional that follows.
- Many families enjoy a tradition of having a special meal on Christmas Eve. Some call it a Joseph and Mary dinner, some a Jerusalem dinner. Others call it a shepherd's dinner or a loaves and fishes dinner. But the idea is basically the same. The menu includes foods that would be typical of the time: broiled fish, lamb, flat bread, hummus, olives, figs, cheese, grape juice, or unsliced loaves of bread that are torn off to eat. Sometimes family members dress in biblical costumes made from bathrobes and other items found around the house. Some families sew costumes to be used from year to year. Spread out a blanket on the floor, turn off all the lights in the house,

and eat by candlelight or old-fashioned lanterns. Play reverent instrumental songs in the background. Afterward, read from the scriptures or have meaningful discussions about the birth of the Savior. Spend the evening reflecting on the humble circumstances into which He was born, how He performed miracles, and how He lived His life.

- Have a Wise Men Night. Children dress as the wise men seeking the Savior, while Joseph and Mary (Dad and Mom) take baby Jesus (a doll) and set up a Nativity scene somewhere in the house, illuminated only by candlelight. The wise men travel throughout the entire house using the star of Bethlehem (flashlight or some kind of lantern). Upon arriving, they kneel around the baby as their parents teach them more about the birth of the Savior, reading from the biblical account. It is unknown how many wise men there really were. Tradition states that there were three because of the three gifts, but there may have been more. This makes an ideal tradition for families of all sizes. If desired, the family could have their Bethlehem meal at this time. Allow children to write down a gift they would like to give to the Savior. Put the slips of paper in unique boxes or ornate containers to symbolize gold, frankincense, and myrrh. Use these as a prominent display in your home to remind them of Bethlehem throughout the season.
- Most families have the tradition of acting out the Nativity on Christmas Eve. Many share this tradition with extended family at a grandparent's home. Parents or grandparents read the scriptures or a written script describing the birth of the Savior as the grandkids act it out. Some families stop at intervals to sing carols during the presentation. You could collect dress-up items to enhance the costumes and allow for more children to participate, or ask the children to think up their own costumes before they come. Children could paint scenery on butcher paper.
- Take pictures of grandchildren while they are dressed up for the Nativity. Attach to foam core boards and cut out. Create your own unique Nativity display to use during the holiday as a delightful reminder of loved ones. Or use the pictures to make your Christmas cards next year. Be creative in taking the photos.

For instance, you could use the shepherds listening to the angel or the wise men on the journey as different themes for the cards.
- Read the scriptures regarding Christ's birth as follows:
  - *Traditional account:* Luke 2:1–20.
  - *Detailed account including Joseph, Herod, and the wise men:* Matthew 1:18–24, Luke 2:1–20, and Matthew 2:1–23.
  - *Book of Mormon account:* 3 Nephi 1:4–23, 26.
  - *Book of Mormon prophecies of Samuel the Lamanite:* Helaman 14:1–12, Helaman 16:1–8, and 3 Nephi 1:4–23, 26.
  - *Combining all the above accounts of His birth, read in the following order:* Helaman 14:1–12; Helaman 16:1–8; Matthew 1:18–24; Luke 2:1–20; 3 Nephi 1:4–23, 26; Matthew 2:1–23.
- If you choose not to act out the Nativity, there are other ways of sharing the story. Parents could read the scriptures and illustrate with pictures from the gospel picture kit or from the meetinghouse library. Or children can put pieces of the Nativity into place at the appropriate times. Other people use flannel board stories, while still others have puppets to use for this occasion.
- Make a slide show presentation with pictures of family members acting out scenes from the Christmas story. Make a soundtrack of scriptures, accompanied by carols. Children could sing some of the songs for the slide show. This would be a great way to preserve family history.
- Have a candle-lit Christmas Eve fireside. Act out the Nativity and read the scriptures and other spiritually uplifting stories. Sing carols or have musical numbers. Family members should all contribute and participate. Use this tender moment to have a testimony meeting with your family. Have a prayer, perhaps kneeling in a circle and holding hands. Take pictures of those participating in the program to put in your Christmas journal or scrapbook. Or videotape the program.
- Read the Sermon on the Mount during the family fireside. Each person writes down a virtue they want to develop during the coming year as a gift to the Savior.
- Allow each member of the family to hold a candle during Christmas Eve devotionals. You can purchase candles and candle

holders, or you can make them by placing a taper candle through a clear disposable cup with an X cut into the bottom. The cup will catch the wax. One person bears his testimony of the Savior and then lights the next person's candle. That person then bears his testimony, and so on, ending with Mother and Father. If desired, this could be done with every person stating something they are thankful for, or a gift they would like to give to the Savior.
- After Christmas Eve devotional, "candle" children to bed. Everyone holds a candle in a procession, and family members sing as they deliver each child, from youngest to oldest, to their beds. As each child is tucked into bed, he blows out his own candle.
- Family members all write an entry in the family journal on Christmas Eve as a keepsake.

CHRISTMAS DAY TRADITIONS

- Wait until Christmas morning to put presents under the Christmas tree. The absence of wrapped presents during the Christmas season could help to reduce the feeling of materialism.
- Fool older children who have a habit of sneaking and opening presents before Christmas. Put an ordinary item in the box to weigh it down, along with a note that there is no peeking allowed.
- Have a contest to see who can guess what their present is. Be creative in coming up with ways to disguise the gift. Tape rattles to the inside of the box, wrap a box inside a box, and so on. Parents could offer scriptural clues to help children guess what their present is.
- Before checking under the tree, children pile into their parents' bed and read the Christmas story together. Afterward, the family members have a nice nutritional breakfast and are then allowed to open their presents.
- Children must go into their parents' room and each sing a favorite Christmas carol before anyone can open presents.
- Dad gathers children from their beds, all the while jingling bells and singing.

- Children must stay in their beds until their parents have called them out of bed by caroling into their bedrooms. Then each child joins the parents in caroling and collecting the next child, until everyone carols into the living room.
- Children gather in the oldest child's room and wait for parents to come to gather them for their Christmas parade. The parade consists of children and parents singing a new carol through each room of the house until they finally reach the living room.
- Children must stay in their beds until they hear music playing. Dad gets up, turns on the tree lights, lights a fire in the fireplace, and puts on the Christmas music to welcome the children.
- Barricade the room that holds the Christmas tree with wrapping paper or other paper to keep children from entering. When parents give the go-ahead, children break through the paper to see the lit tree with presents waiting.
- On Christmas morning, read the First Presidency's Christmas message from the *Ensign* magazine and have a family prayer before opening presents.
- Open gifts one at a time so that everyone can see what is being received, starting with the youngest and ending with the oldest.
- After waking, family members kneel on chairs that have been placed with their backs to the table the night before, and have a heartfelt Christmas morning prayer. They then have a nice breakfast before moving into the living room.
- Children must prepare and serve their parents a nice breakfast before they may open their presents.
- Have a breakfast brunch for extended family on Christmas Day. Dad is in charge and gives Mom a break for Christmas.
- Take a Christmas breakfast basket to an elderly couple or a neighbor. Include delicious breakfast cake, some hot chocolate, perhaps a new tree ornament, and some pretty Christmas napkins.
- Instead of having an expensive formal Christmas dinner, have a picnic on the floor by the Christmas tree with finger foods and pie. Then donate the saved money to a charity that feeds the hungry, or deliver the groceries you would have used to someone in need.

- Invite neighbors, friends, or ward members who have no family gatherings to have Christmas dinner with your family.
- Hold an open house Christmas night for your extended family. Invite others to help with the refreshments, since most people have extra treats that they are willing to share. Play games, watch home movies, or just enjoy each other's company.

CHAPTER 9

serve one another

Service has always been the defining character trait of our Savior Jesus Christ. It is His doctrine to be charitable, compassionate, and full of love for one another. He provided us with the perfect example of love by laying down His life for us. All He asks in return is that we become His disciples and follow Him. He said, "He that believeth on me, the works that I do shall He do also" (John 14:12).

On the shores of the Sea of Tiberias, the Savior taught His disciples this principle. Twice He asked Peter if he loved Him, and each time Peter replied that he did. Both times, the Savior's response was the same: "Feed my sheep." Then once again, Jesus inquired, "Simon, son of Jonas, lovest thou me?" This time, Peter was grieved because he had already answered the question. He replied, "Lord, thou knowest all things; thou knowest that I love thee," only to hear for the third time, "Feed my sheep." The repetition of this phrase witnesses to the world the importance of His directive—not only to the disciples of old but to those who would ever hope to be a disciple.

Do we ever get annoyed, like Peter, when we are told yet again to feed His sheep—to serve one another? We've all heard the importance of this commandment time and time again to the point that we may feel like saying, "Yes, Lord, I heard you already." But too often we listen with one ear while our thoughts wander to all that we have on our to-do list.

OPPORTUNITIES ARE PERISHABLE

If we are not too busy and distracted elsewhere, we will find that there are opportunities all around us to serve others—not only at Christmas but throughout the year as well. Each act of charity on our part will give us another chance to bring Christ into our hearts and into our lives. If we fail to expand our view to see the limitless chances around us to serve, we will miss out on some of life's greatest joys.

Like Christ admonishing the disciples of old to feed His sheep, in our day it is President Monson who speaks to us about availing ourselves of these chances to serve. We have watched him devote his life to service as a bishop and later as a General Authority. He personifies what Christmas is all about, and many times he has counseled us that our opportunities to give of ourselves are limitless; but they are also perishable.

Time passes so quickly, on wings of lightning, we are told. A famous author once said, "I expect to pass through this world but once. Any good work, therefore, any kindness, or any service I can render to any soul of man or animal, let me do it now! Let me not neglect or defer it, for I shall not pass this way again."

We often see others whose acts of service seem second nature to them. These people, we observe, seem to have mastered the art of being mindful of the needs of other people. Rather than lamenting lost opportunities for charity or kindness, they move from "good intention" to "opportunity taken." It appears that their acts of kindness have become equal to the righteous desires of their hearts.

How do we master this art of awareness so that we are sensitive to the needs of those around us? This skill takes a lifetime to master, and in essence it is the art of living the gospel fully. I believe that we often think about the amount of work that service entails and shy away from putting ourselves into action because we are already overwhelmed with life. It just becomes too much at times.

IN WISDOM AND ORDER

The answer does not lie in picking up our pace or running faster than we have strength. King Benjamin has given us this advice: "And see that all these things are done in wisdom and order; for it is not requisite that a man should run faster than he has strength. And again, it is expedient that he should be diligent, that thereby he might win the prize; therefore, all things must be done in order" (Mosiah 4:27).

I often hear people applying this scripture to the pace of life in general. If we are organized and orderly, if we use our day planners effectively, if we prioritize our tasks, if we make use of every minute of our day, and if we take care of our bodies, then we will have the strength do more and more with our time. But that interpretation is taken slightly out of context if we read the previous verse: "And now, for the sake of these things which I have spoken unto you—that is, for the sake of retaining a remission of your sins from day to day, that ye may walk guiltless before God—I would that ye should impart of your substance to the poor, every man according to that which he hath, such as feeding the hungry, clothing the naked, visiting the sick, and administering to their relief, both spiritually and temporally, according to their wants" (Mosiah 4:26).

King Benjamin had been referring to what we must do to retain a remission of our sins—that we must have charity. In order to walk guiltless, it is expedient that we are diligent in exercising charity. He tells us specifically what we need to do, but even if we were to feed the hungry, clothe the naked, and visit the sick every waking moment of every day, there would still be so much more to do. We would easily become overwhelmed by the countless opportunities to serve, and it is in this regard that he counsels us to not run faster than we have strength. The Lord does not expect us to do more than we can reasonably do with the other responsibilities that we have, hence the directive to have wisdom and order in choosing our priorities.

THERE IS A SEASON

There are seasons in our lives when we will not have the strength to administer to the relief of others. A mother expecting a baby may be too ill to do much of anything. Perhaps another woman, although she is willing, cannot serve as much as she'd like because of chronic illness or another physical limitation. I have been in that position before, and I was grieved because I could not serve others as I wanted to. Perhaps we don't feel that we have the means to do what we want to do. In these moments, we should remember King Benjamin's words: "I would that ye say in your hearts that: I give not because I have not, but if I had I would give" (Mosiah 4:24).

WE MUST LISTEN IN ORDER TO HEAR

Our ability to serve effectively is dependent upon our ability to listen and to hear and the ability to discern the gift of the Holy Ghost. Terri Cannavo, in her book *So You're Not Mother Teresa*, says,

> Are you aware that the word *listen* contains the same letters as the word *silent*? This is a significant indicator to the kind of listening that needs to take place when you are giving yourself to others in need. . . .
>
> To become an effective listener, you must seek silence in your world, which promotes stillness inside of you. This stillness is the receptive center for hearing your impressions. Use stillness and quiet to your advantage. There will be lulls in a conversation. Listen to any promptings or impressions you are being given. You may receive important information in this silence with specific guidance on how to help this grieving individual in front of you. Trust these impressions implicitly. Act on them quickly if they are counseling action.[1]

Some people say that because they have not experienced dreams and visions, they have not experienced the gift of the Holy Ghost. More likely, they have not yet learned how to perceive and interpret the smallest of promptings that come their way.

In *Spiritual Survival in the Last Days*, Blaine and Brenton Yorgason explain that we often don't hear promptings from the Holy Ghost:

> We have come to the conclusion that we all have certain abilities within us that might be called spiritual muscles. And like physical muscles, these spiritual muscles grow stronger with exercises designed to enhance their growth and ultimate power. . . . We can grow into the principle of personal revelation. However, most of us have probably been prompted by the Holy Ghost much more often than we might imagine. In fact, we may grow old and die before we finally learn how frequently the Spirit has helped us and guided us in our lives.[2]

By becoming more familiar with the workings of the Holy Ghost and calling upon it more often, we will be led more frequently to those opportunities to serve until service becomes a way of life for us. I love the following quote from Marion G. Romney: "Service is not something we endure on this earth so we can earn the right to live in the celestial kingdom. Service is the very fiber of which an exalted life in the celestial kingdom is made."[3]

SERVE TOGETHER AS A FAMILY

Some of my favorite and most profound memories are serving with my family. I remember, for example, the look on my son's face when, as a five-year-old child, he helped deliver a modest little tree that we purchased and decorated for a neighbor who didn't have money for one. As the door opened, all of a sudden he spontaneously began singing with gusto, "We Wish You a Merry Christmas." I will never forget the excited, sweet demeanor of that little boy as he gave his heart away along with that much-appreciated Christmas tree.

Another year, the father of my daughter's best friend lost his job just before Christmas. My daughter was desperate to help her friend somehow, so she asked us if she could give their family some food. We took her to the store and gave her the last fifty dollars of our food budget and a calculator, with the charge to make every penny count. Although she was only twelve years old, she went about the task with great determination and was able to buy an amazing amount of food. She placed it all into a large decorated box and left it on their doorstep. Then she rang the bell and ran to the car where we were waiting. I remember how she beamed with the happiness and satisfaction that comes only from sacrificing on behalf of someone else. Experiences like that become etched in your heart and in your memory.

On another occasion, I planned a small activity to let my boys have some fun decorating cookies, while providing them with a chance to serve. I made a huge batch of gingerbread dough and let our two sons, ages ten and twelve, invite some friends to come over and help make cookies. The six boys rolled out the dough, baked, and decorated dozens of eight-inch gingerbread men. They had a great time as they chattered, laughed, and made jokes all afternoon.

After they had wrapped all the gingerbread men, we took them to a nursing home, where we had arranged to deliver the cookies to the residents. As these cute little boys went room by room and took turns handing out little gingerbread men, they were surprised how such a small gift, given from their hearts, could bring tears to nearly every one of the sweet elderly men and women. Many of these residents hadn't received even a single visitor during that Christmas season, and so a single gingerbread man meant the world to those so burdened by loneliness. When we left, the boys' eyes were filled with tears, and their hearts were full of joy, as was mine. The activity took only one afternoon but provided a lifetime of memories for all of us.

Service affects children in extraordinary ways. Due to their innocence, they tend to be far more susceptible to the influence of the Holy Ghost. However, as they grow older, they are faced with tremendous social pressures to be sarcastic, mean, and biting. By helping our children practice the skill of serving others from a young age, we firmly establish the character traits that will continue to adulthood and will ultimately help them overcome the greediness and selfishness so rampant in the world today.

If we as parents do not use the Christmas season to teach our children about selfless service, then we are missing out on some of the greatest opportunities to thwart Satan in the battle for the souls of our children. Childhood lasts but a moment, and we must not give up that moment. We can gear our service activities and our family experiences to our children's abilities to serve, even if it is only by baking some simple gingerbread men. Through even the humblest act of service performed by a child, we will witness the miracle and wonder of Christmas as their true selfless identities begin to unfold before our very eyes.

GIVE THE GIFT OF SELF

We can teach children by example, we can provide opportunities for them, and we can show them how wonderful it feels to serve others. But before we can be examples, we must first take the time and effort to put ourselves into action to answer the call to serve. John A. Widtsoe said that giving to the Lord should come first, even before our families. "It is easy to give to our own, those whom we love. Their gladness becomes our joy. We are not quite so ready to give to others, even if they are in need, for their happiness does not seem so necessary to our happiness. . . . We have foolishly reversed the proper order. Our first gift at Christmas should be to the Lord; next to the friend or stranger by our gate; then, surcharged with the effulgence from such giving, we would enhance the value of our gifts to our very own."[4] Stated another way, we should follow the JOY principle in setting the priorities in our lives. That is, Jesus first, Others second, Yourself last.

I have learned that when we invest ourselves by serving others, we receive an overwhelming return on our "investment." We tend to find more peace and satisfaction in what we are doing, and we tend to put things in their proper perspective. Does it matter if we have to clean up the kitchen after six little boys if they walk away, as Brother Widtsoe stated, "surcharged with the effulgence" from such giving? Effulgence is defined as a "brightness or a light radiating from something." That truly is the power of service, an increase in the light we radiate. And everyone around us will benefit from this radiating light of the Spirit, if we but give our "heart and a willing mind" (D&C 64:34).

Before I was married, I had high ambitions of what it meant to help those in need. I believed that I needed to perform a grand and noble act of service, some saving of mankind, so to speak. I wanted to change the world, and as such I wanted to serve in the Peace Corps or a similar group where I could reach out to lands beyond my own to ease suffering.

But then life happened, and as a wife and mother, I learned the simplicities of serving. I learned that service is not about one grand act of worthwhile endeavor. It is about thousands of everyday random acts of kindness, and the most effective service begins at home. Everyone can do small things if their hearts are willing and not distracted by the world. Elder Richard L. Evans has said, "We can't do everything for everyone everywhere, but we can do something for someone somewhere."[5]

Outside of my role as wife and mother, I also need to safeguard my own heart against worldliness and the tendency to selfishness. Many years ago I committed to give a gift to the Savior every year. I felt that it needed to be a very personal thing that would require sacrifice on my part. As David said, "neither will I offer burnt offerings unto the Lord my God of that which doth cost me nothing" (2 Samuel 24:24). This has become my most important gift every season because I have learned from experience that when we give of ourselves to the Lord first, then we are of more value to our families, just as Brother Widtsoe testified.

I have also learned that service does not have to be expensive or time-consuming. We don't have to go to Africa; we only have to go down the street. We don't have to spend a lot of money or a lot of time to make an impact on someone's life.

This lesson hit home for me one year when I was very busy being a full-time mom and student. I was so overwhelmed with the list of "absolutely must do's" that I had not even thought about my gift to the Lord. I was disappointed in myself because for several years I had made this my highest priority.

With Christmas less than a week away, I had driven to the grocery store at about 11:00 PM to pick up a few necessities. I had been feeling bad that time had become such a slave master to me that year, and I truly needed a small dose of Christmas happiness. Before going into the store, I bowed my head and pleaded with the Lord to guide me to just one act of service, something small but a sacrifice nonetheless, that I could do in the short amount of time I had.

As I came out of the store, my eyes caught sight of an isolated car in the corner of the large parking lot. The Spirit whispered to me that someone in that car needed my help. I drove closer, and in the freezing December weather, I saw a frightened elderly woman sitting in the car alone. Her breath had turned to ice on the windows, but when I asked if I could help her, she yelled at me to go away. It took some time to convince her that I was not a criminal (although apparently I must have looked like one, because she was terrified). I continued to reassure her that I only wanted to help her. Her car had stalled and died, and with no way home, she had been sitting there for hours in the cold, too frightened in the dark to even walk back to the store.

When I told her that I could drive her home, she refused and said her son could come for her in the morning when he got off of work. Maybe she wasn't thinking very clearly due to hypothermia, but she had decided the best thing to do was to stay in that car until morning. After some time, she realized I wasn't going anywhere without her, so she finally allowed me to drive her home, which was at least a thirty-minute drive. She was nervous, cold, and apprehensive, but she managed to utter a sincere thanks as she left the warmth of my car.

On the way home, I shed tears of gratitude that my Father in Heaven had helped me serve someone, even though it was a small, random act of service late at night. I had needed to feel a little bit of Christmas joy, and that one insignificant hour that I gave up to help someone else was the best hour I spent that entire Christmas season. It brought me an abundance of joy, for which I was deeply grateful. "Give," said Jesus, "and it shall be given unto you; good measure, pressed down, and shaken together, and running over" (Luke 6:38).

People often need our help at inconvenient times, but we must be available to fill a need whenever those needs exist. If we construct our days so tightly and our schedules so fixed that we can't spare a little time when opportunities come our way to serve (and they will), we may feel so frustrated and irritated that we resent the chance to serve and consider it a burden.

When we take the time to still our hearts, we become receptive to what the moment has to offer us. If we will listen, Christmas will speak to our hearts. When we become accustomed to feeling the influence of the Holy Ghost, the Lord will show us what we should do, and it will become so natural to us that we may not even notice that we are listening. And as He did with me in the parking lot of that store, He will even teach us when to pray and what to say so that we will become more spiritually in tune and receptive. It was not a coincidence that I went shopping to that store at that hour—He was reaching out to help a frightened elderly woman make it through the night. Small miracles will work together, and all of a sudden we will realize that God has granted us the opportunity to be his angels on Earth.

THERE ARE ANGELS AMONG US

On another occasion, I witnessed many miracles coming together to help a family who had moved into our ward. The father was completing his long-awaited schooling, they had nine children, and they lived on a meager amount of money. It was just before Christmas, and their three-year-old daughter had to be admitted to a hospital to remove an abdominal growth. I didn't know them very well, but I was going to visit my grandmother in the same hospital, which was located several hours away. I decided to stop by the little girl's room and see if there was anything I could do for this girl and her family.

Before I left, I mentioned to my mother during a phone call that I was a little hesitant to visit without a gift. She told me she had felt prompted the previous week to make an extra Cabbage Patch doll when she was sewing some for her granddaughters and that I could drop by to pick it up if I wanted to take it to the hospital. She had done a great job—it looked just like the real deal. It had a plastic head and yarn hair, with a stuffed body, and the girl would never know that it wasn't an expensive one from the store. I thanked my mom, quickly stuffed the doll into a gift bag that was a bit too small, and went on my way. I was grateful to have something to give to this little girl.

When I walked into the hospital room, both of her parents were there, and when they turned and saw me, they both started to cry as if on cue. I didn't know what to do, but the mother motioned to me to sit by her as she explained.

She told me that they had gone to the hospital in a rush and didn't have time to think about taking her teddy bear with them. All the other children had something to cuddle, and when their daughter was inconsolable and frightened after her difficult surgery, she had begged and pleaded for her bear. The parents couldn't return to their home several hours away to get it, and they didn't have any money to buy a new one.

It was very difficult for them to see their daughter suffer, and they had prayed about how to help ease her pain. Not long after that, I walked in the door holding a gift bag with a Cabbage Patch doll poking her little plastic head up out of the bag (they could immediately tell what it was), and they knew that God had heard and answered their prayers.

The interesting part was that the only thing their daughter could talk about for months before Christmas was how much she wanted a Cabbage Patch doll, and they knew they wouldn't have the money to buy her one. This was an answer to their prayers as their little girl reached out and hugged that little doll for all she was worth.

The outpouring of love from Heavenly Father did not stop there. As I visited with her parents, it became obvious that they were worried about their eight other children they had left at home. They hadn't had the chance to do any shopping and now they wouldn't have any money. They didn't have a tree, and they wouldn't even be able to buy anything for stockings.

I returned home and the next day I received a phone call from a woman who ran a daycare center across the street from my home. They were finished with school for the year and wanted to know if I knew of anyone who could use their decorated Christmas tree. Someone else phoned that night—did I know anyone who could use some extra help this Christmas? The next day, I saw the ward Primary president, who asked me if I knew anyone who could use all the extra oranges, nuts, and candy that were left over from their Christmas party. Then I ran into the bishop, and he had some ideas about how the ward could help. With all that, plus some clothing that I was able to arrange for the kids, Christmas was ready when the parents brought their daughter home on Christmas Eve.

A lot of little miracles came together, and a lot of receptive people had listened to the promptings of the Spirit on that family's behalf. President Spencer W. Kimball spoke this oft-quoted thought: "God does notice us, and he watches over us. But it is usually through another person that he meets our needs. Therefore, it is vital that we serve each other in the kingdom. . . . So often, our acts of service consist of simple encouragement or of giving mundane help with mundane tasks, but what glorious consequences can flow from mundane acts and from small but deliberate deeds!"[6]

We must never discount how important small acts are. We often cannot see that our small part is being enlarged by the combined acts of God's angels here on earth. I am grateful for the opportunity to play a small part in helping this family. I could have missed the chance if there had not been enough time in my own schedule to practice a random act of kindness by visiting a little girl.

GOD BLESSES EVEN THE SMALLEST EFFORT

Gingerbread men, Cabbage Patch dolls, and giving someone a ride home may not seem very important in the overall scheme of things. But I have shared these examples because they all have one thing in common: they are small, insignificant, seemingly unimportant experiences that just by chance happened to leave me with memories I would never trade. The enlargement of the heart that comes from an act of simple service comes to us by our willingness and our desire to help, not by the size of our pocketbook or the scope of the project.

Our Father in Heaven is willing and ready to bless us in our smallest attempts at serving his sheep, even if all we do is make a gingerbread man. He will pour out joy to fill our hearts and give us the peace that we so desire.

Following are examples of ways to serve, given with the hope that readers will be able to find some form of giving that will enhance their Christmas celebration. Adapt these ideas according to your strength and capacity to serve. Remember, do not run faster than you have strength, especially at Christmastime!

Notes
1. Terri Cannavo, *So You're Not Mother Teresa* (Dallas: Brown Books Publishing Group, 2006), 27, 33.
2. Blaine and Brenton Yorgason, *Spiritual Survival in the Last Days*, (Salt Lake City: Deseret Book, 1990), 188.
3. President Marion G. Romney, "The Celestial Nature of Self-reliance, *Ensign*, Nov. 1982, 91.
4. Elder John A. Widtsoe, "The Gifts of Christmas," *Ensign*, Dec. 1972, 4. (Originally appeared in the *Improvement Era*, vol. 28 [1935], 752)
5. Elder Richard L. Evans, *Richard Evans' Quote Book* (Salt Lake City: Publisher's Press, 1978), 239.
6. *The Teachings of Spencer W. Kimball* (Salt Lake City: Bookcraft, 1982), 252.

IDEAS FOR
serving
ONE ANOTHER

● ● ● ● ● ● ● ● ● ● ●

TEACHING CHILDREN TO SERVE

Many service projects in other categories are appropriate for the entire family, but children also need to have their own opportunities to sacrifice on behalf of others, not only at Christmas, but throughout the year.

- During the year, children can save up money in their own Christmas Jar. Small amounts of change go into the jar all year, and the money is used at Christmas to help the less fortunate. As per the book *The Christmas Jar*, anonymously deliver the jar just the way it is or purchase something to be given anonymously to someone in need. Begin your new jar on New Year's Day.
- Organize a free babysitting service for members of the ward who would like to do some Christmas shopping without children. Announce the service in church for a couple of weeks. Arrange the details about the location and what types of games, activities, toys, and snacks will be offered to entertain the children. Set a time limit and be sure to get emergency contact information from the parents.
- Organize a book drive and collect new and gently used books to donate to Sub-for-Santa, shelters, safe houses, libraries, or schools. Do a little research and decide who could use your help. Then conduct a drive in your ward or neighborhood.
- Make arrangements to provide bishopric members with finger foods or sandwiches during tithing settlement in December. They put in long hours and are sometimes underappreciated for their service.
- Show appreciation for other ward members who provide valuable services but are underappreciated, such as the ward

clerk or the librarian. Take them a plate of goodies with a sincere thank-you note.
- Even very young children can help make a meal and deliver it to someone in need. Let them have firsthand knowledge of what it feels like to serve another person.
- Children can bake and deliver plates of cookies to neighbors and friends with only a little encouragement and supervision from parents. Encourage children to make at least one plate to take to someone they do not know very well or to think of someone they wouldn't normally choose who might really appreciate the gift.
- Encourage older children to purchase a modest Christmas tree along with some lights and decorations. Decorate the tree and then deliver it to a family who doesn't have money for a tree. Ask your bishop if he has any suggestions. Students who are using all their resources to go to school, single mothers, or families whose parents are serving in a military deployment are all good choices. Plan to do this fairly early in the season so that if the family has already purchased a tree, you could give it to someone else (ask them if they know of anyone else who may need a tree). Or give it anonymously by placing it on the step and hiding in the yard—you won't want to miss the delightful reaction.
- Teenagers can plan a snowman contest, snowball war, or another outdoor activity to occupy younger children while parents do much-needed Christmas tasks.
- Sponsor a birthday party for Jesus. Bake and decorate a cake and invite neighborhood children. Have them bring an inexpensive but well-made item to donate to Sub-for-Santa. Then have a piece of cake, sing some songs, and enjoy spending time with the children.
- Give small surprises to someone in need of cheering up for the twelve days of Christmas.
- Consider doing acts of service for the twelve days of Christmas. These don't have to be big things in order to touch a heart. Start by making breakfast for your family.
- Present a gift certificate for babysitting to a young couple with children so that they can have a night out at the temple.
- Adopt a grandparent from among the elderly in your neighborhood and secretly do something nice for him or her.

Sign everything "Merry Christmas from a secret grandchild."
- Visit children in hospitals. Help them make a few Christmas cards or small gifts for their families. Read to them, sing with them, and enjoy being with them.
- Get together with friends and go caroling to a nursing home resident. Ask the supervisor beforehand if caroling is allowed and if there is someone in particular who could use a little cheering up. Take along a decorated miniature tree for your new friend.
- Get together with a group of friends and conduct a service scavenger hunt as a Christmas party. Divide into teams, and with an assigned number of tasks you must do, go to neighbors' homes and ask to perform one act of service of their choosing, such as cleaning a sink or reading to the young child. Upon returning, have some yummy Christmas treats and hot chocolate and share your experiences.
- Be a "Christmas angel" to a single mother or father by taking the children shopping to help them select a gift for their parent. Offer to help tend the children so the parent can have some time for errands, to go to the temple, or just have a break for a few hours.
- Go to the grocery store and purchase food for a family in need. Set a dollar limit and pick out some fun foods that the family can't afford, or stick with practical food that everyone can use. Decorate and fill a large box. Then anonymously put it on their doorstep and watch with delight from a distance.
- Help someone less fortunate by putting some money or a gift card into an envelope and sending it in the mail or delivering it anonymously. This could be done by a third party who can explain that they have been asked to help deliver a gift from someone who cares.
- Take up a collection of useful items to give to the local missionaries. These can be food items such as a boxed skillet meal, mini boxes of cereal, granola bars, fruit snacks, Christmas candy, chocolate oranges, toiletries, toilet paper, or anything else that might be useful. Spend an evening wrapping every item separately. Then put them into a box with a bow or into a large stocking. Choose whether one gift should be opened every day during the month of December, or if the missionaries have to wait until Christmas morning and open all of them at once.
- Write a letter to a missionary serving from the ward, or send a

package of homemade cookies, if possible.
- Send a letter or drawing to someone who would appreciate it. Organizations such as Make a Child Smile (makeachildsmile.org) or Hugs and Hope (hugsandhope.org) invite children to send cards or letters to sick children across the country. Or they can give drawings and pictures to local nursing homes or Meals on Wheels services to include with food deliveries. The group Color a Smile (colorasmile.org) also collects children's drawings to give away to similar groups.
- A national effort such as The Box Project (boxproject.org) operates year round, letting volunteers pick families to help by sending monthly boxes of food, clothes, and other needed items. In many cases, you can get to know these families by writing letters.
- Through efforts like The Binky Patrol (binkypatrol.org), families can work with a simple pattern and some fleece to knot together inexpensive snuggly blankets, which are sent to homeless shelters or to children and teens in need of comfort.
- Another group, Warm Up America, has volunteers nationwide who knit sections that are joined into afghans for the homeless. The website (warmupamerica.org) has simple patterns for beginners and instructions.
- Make and donate kits through LDS Humanitarian Services. Personal hygiene kits, newborn kits, or school kits can be assembled, or other items can be donated, such as quilts, first-aid items, new children's clothing, crib sheets, knitted or crocheted hats and mittens, toys, puppets, dolls, and file folder games. Guidelines and instructions for these and others can also be found under Humanitarian Services at www.providentliving.org or www.lds.org.
- When hosting holiday parties, ask each guest to bring a gift that can be given to a less-fortunate child. Mark the appropriate age and gender on the package.

HOMELESS SHELTERS AND SUPPORT CENTERS

Find a way to give to the homeless without putting anyone in harm's way. Be cautious if you ever invite someone you don't know into your home. You could invite the person to join you at a restaurant for a warm meal instead.

- Give to a Family Support Center. These exist in many communities, and there is an ongoing need for help. Call in advance to offer your time and efforts. There may be a specific need that isn't obvious. They may ask for help with food instead of clothing, for instance.
- Give to those who live on the streets. You could make care packages containing food items that don't need to be cooked and clothing such as coats, gloves, hats, flannel shirts, or small blankets.
- Learn about local homeless shelters in the community. Donate food, clothing, and blankets, or make personal hygiene kits. Other items that are often needed include sheets, towels, toys, books, and disposable diapers. Have children help deliver the donation.
- Volunteer to help prepare or serve food at a local shelter.
- Often, homeless shelters are in need of help with young children. Volunteer to read stories or tutor them in basic reading and math skills, or take them on a Christmas outing.
- Make a donation to the homeless shelter, asking children in the family to contribute to the cause as well. They will be more willing to help if they have previously had the opportunity to serve the homeless, such as helping on Thanksgiving.
- Buy gift cards from a big chain store (the kind that have both household goods and groceries). Put the gift cards into Christmas cards, and write something like, "We've been so blessed by our loving Savior, and we would like to honor Him by giving this to you. May the Lord bless you. Merry Christmas." Sign the card, "Someone who cares."
- Go for a drive and pray that you will find someone who needs some help. When you are prompted to do so, roll down the window and say, "You don't know us, but we would like to give you a gift. Merry Christmas!"
- Help children organize a neighborhood drive to collect items that are in demand at a local shelter or for another cause. Possibilities are mittens, gently used coats, hats, or used baby blankets. Children should pass out flyers explaining that they are trying to collect for a personal service project and will return in a week to see if the neighbor would like to donate items for the needy.
- Make fleece blankets and donate them to a local battered women's shelter. Teddy bears or other cuddly stuffed animals are also always appreciated.

- Ask children to donate one of their new Christmas toys to a shelter, or have them earn the money to buy some small toys with their own money. Young children are often willing to donate their used toys, but make sure that the toys are in excellent shape.

HELPING OTHERS IN THE NEIGHBORHOOD OR WARD

I recommend consulting with your bishop since there may already be someone helping the family that you have decided to help. He may also know if there really is a need. Many people prefer to have a more modest Christmas. Some good friends of mine found themselves in this position one year when they were given many boxes of gifts for their family. There were toys, clothing, home goods, groceries, newly made quilts, and a refurbished computer. However, it was the very year that they had made the decision as a family to enjoy a modest Christmas, and they were very disappointed.

If you find yourself in the position to help another family, pray about who really needs the help. The Lord will lead you to where you need to go. But if you find yourself on the receiving side and have been given more than you really need, I suggest that you turn around and find someone else who truly is in need and have your family participate in giving to them. Or if you have been given items that do not fit into your simplified gift-giving plan, just quietly put them away for another day. Spread out the kindness you have been given over the coming year. It won't lessen the kindness of the giver or the worth of the present. Then thank the Lord that you have been given such generous gifts.

- Team up with other families to be a Secret Santa for an individual or a family in the ward.
- Secretly deliver treats or gifts to someone in your neighborhood who needs a little Christmas joy.
- Secretly shovel the snow off a neighbor's driveway early in the morning or late at night when they aren't watching or are not at home.
- Donate money to the LDS Church Humanitarian Services through a local ward or branch, or by sending a check to Humanitarian Services, 50 East North Temple Street, Floor 7, Salt Lake City, UT 84150-6890. Donations may also be made online through www.providentliving.org. If you have more time than money, you can assemble kits and other needed items

in the humanitarian services rooms in select Deseret Industries locations. All materials are supplied for the projects. See above websites for locations.

FOOD DRIVES

- Make kits of baking supplies to give to those who might not have the money to spend on luxuries. Include the basics along with a few extra things, such as decorating sprinkles and nuts.
- Prepare jars of layered cookie mixes to give to those families that have several children and may not have the means to buy the extras.
- A good way to donate to the food bank is to call ahead and ask what types of items they need the most. Every time you go to the grocery store, pick up one or two of the items, and give children the responsibility of collecting the food into a box. When the boxes are full, have children help deliver the box to the food bank. Then begin filling another box.
- Volunteer at your local food bank. Help sort food and stack shelves; sometimes delivery drivers are needed as well.
- Help children conduct a food drive in the neighborhood for something the local food bank specifically needs, such as cans of soup. Most neighbors are happy to donate to service projects that young children are involved with. Children then take the donated items to the food bank.
- Prepare a food box for a nice Christmas Eve dinner. Include a frozen turkey, stuffing, a bag of potatoes, olives, cranberry sauce, and so on. Deliver to a low-income family or homebound seniors living on fixed incomes. Give a turkey breast for small families to prevent waste.
- Transport food to those in need. Many stores and restaurants will give away good food that has passed its expiration date, but these must be delivered to the needy or to a shelter. Help is also needed by certain agencies to deliver food to low-income families.

My stepfather was a kind man with a big heart. He was always giving time, money, or food to anyone who needed it. In the last years of his life, he transported day-old bread from a grocery store every day to many people around town who needed the help. His favorite way to help others was to buy fruit trees for couples with young children and little money. He must have bought hundreds. He and his generous heart have been missed by many, including myself!

- Contact Meals on Wheels to see if they need assistance delivering food during the month of December. Sometimes regulars need some time to take care of their own Christmas needs and will welcome substitutes.
- Take leftover holiday candy to correction centers or shelters.
- Send out for pizza and have it delivered to a family as a surprise.
- Instead of taking in a meal to a family that you know could use the help, buy gift certificates for a local grocery store or restaurant. These are especially helpful if family members have dietary restrictions.
- Fill a large box with basic pantry foods. Cover in wrapping paper and take to the Relief Society president who can deliver it to a needy family.
- Prepare sack lunches and drive to an area of town where you know there is a definite need. Deliver them to homeless people or take them to a shelter to be handed out.

CLOTHING DRIVES

I recently read a short story written by a woman riding on a bus who saw an elderly woman rubbing her cold hands together. She wondered why society does not help those in need. As she pondered on this, a young man exiting the bus passed the elderly woman, and as he did, he gently took off and placed his black gloves on her lap. This story moved me because it demonstrates how even the smallest thing can make a big difference. I have resolved to carry a pair of new gloves with me with the hope that I, too, can make a tiny difference. When I feel them in my pocket, they will remind me to listen for the sound of His sandaled feet.

- Take the time to clean out your coat closet and give some warm winter clothing to those who really need it. Make it a tradition to give away your coat every time you buy a new one. It could be donated to a shelter or given personally to someone who needs one.
- Many children go to school every day without a coat, gloves, or hats. Sponsor a drive to collect these items for the children. Contact the PTA for help and possible suggestions.

- Start a collection drive for gently used shoes or eyeglasses to be given to a developing country. Contact social agencies to find out where to send the items, or research online.
- Prepare "Welcome Baby" kits that contain the basics for newborns and give them to low-income mothers.

SERVE THE ELDERLY OR DISABLED

Loneliness is sometimes more painful than poverty. The elderly, sick, or bereaved often long for someone just to talk with. They want visits more than presents, so give them the gift of your time. Often, nursing home residents never have a visitor the entire Christmas season. We shouldn't allow that to happen!

- Offer to sign and address Christmas cards for someone who is elderly, blind, or disabled.
- Help senior citizens who live alone by offering to decorate their Christmas tree or to set up and take down Christmas decorations for them.
- Offer to run errands for senior citizens. Help with grocery shopping, errands, or picking up a prescription. Offer to drive them to appointments. This is especially helpful for those who no longer drive. If they have pets, offer to take them for a walk or to the vet.
- Take a warm loaf of bread and some jam or honey butter to an elderly neighbor.
- Offer to provide respite care to families coping with the stress of providing full-time care for the disabled. Give them the opportunity to finish their Christmas shopping.
- Pay for professional cleaners to go into the home of the elderly. They will more likely allow a stranger to clean their home than someone they know.
- Adopt a grandparents from the neighborhood and learn as much as you can about them. Ask them about their Christmas memories. Take them out to see holiday lights, go Christmas shopping for them, or take them to a Christmas concert. Fill a Christmas stocking for them. Invite them to come to your home for Christmas dinner.
- Adopt a nursing home grandparent. Contact the supervisor to ask for names of residents who are not likely to receive a visitor,

and arrange an appropriate time to visit. Visit every day for the twelve days of Christmas and read a moving Christmas story each day. Decorate his room for Christmas. Give your nursing home grandparent a small gift and treats if his diet is not restricted. Appropriate gifts include a cozy fleece blanket, new pajamas, socks or slippers, toiletries, or a new face towel.

- Call the director of a local nursing home and ask for the names of several people who don't often receive mail. Send each a Christmas card, and sign it "from someone who cares."
- Many people make it an annual custom to visit a nursing home to present a Christmas program. Join with a few other families and prepare some musical numbers and a few short stories. Call the nursing home and schedule a time for your program.

SEEK OUT THE LONELY

- Seek out someone who is alone during the holidays and ask him to celebrate with your family. Invite him to come to Christmas Eve or Christmas dinner, and include him in your family traditions.
- Seek out extended family members who need to know that someone cares about them. Take the time to visit and give them a treat, such as a tin of homemade candy or something else that indicates your sincerity. You may also choose to do silent acts of service for them.
- Make an effort to call and cheer friends during the Christmas season if they are grieving or have lost a family member during the past year. The first year alone at Christmas can be devastating. Take them an unexpected meal to show that you care.
- Invite a foreign student to share Christmas dinner with you. See if a local university offers programs designed to pair up host families with international students over the Christmas holiday. These students are far from home and family, and this can be a great opportunity to learn more about people from other countries, along with their customs and traditions.
- Adopt a refugee family for Christmas. When these families first become established, they usually have very few possessions. Providing Christmas for them helps them to feel more welcome in a foreign land.

- Share supper and seasonal scriptures with a stranger, such as someone who is undergoing treatment at a nearby children's hospital, someone who can't get home for the holidays, or someone who does not usually celebrate Christmas customs. If you live close to a military installation, invite a military member and his family to be your guest for a meal.
- Send a Christmas card or a care package to a soldier. These usually have to be done early so they can be distributed in time. There are many organizations that help support soldiers.
- Give a little something back by surprising a public servant on Christmas Eve or Christmas Day. Take cookies or other treats to firefighters, EMTs, or police officers. Too often, we don't think about those who give up their Christmases to serve the community. Call city government offices for more information.

SPONTANEOUS AND RANDOM ACTS OF SERVICE

Be prepared to offer help whenever it is needed. Watch and observe for a need that you might fill. Pray about opportunities that will fit into your schedule, and leave room in your day so that you have time to do something random and spontaneous.

- Offer to take a single mother out for lunch, to a Christmas concert, or to another function.
- Find a family with young children and offer to carpool children to school, sports, Christmas concerts, and so forth.
- Anonymously pick up the tab of the person behind you at a tollbooth or movie theater, and spread the Christmas feeling of kindness and charity.
- Give the gift of life. Donate a pint of blood.
- Talk to a good friend about the Church and ask if he would like to come to your home to hear the missionary discussions.
- Get tickets to a special Christmas concert or performance and give them to someone who couldn't otherwise afford to go.
- Greet the mailman with a donut and a cup of hot chocolate.
- Do something to help a stranger with no expectation of something in return.

RESOURCES FOR SERVICE OPPORTUNITIES

A good resource for service opportunities is the website www.About.com, where a list is posted of the current Top 5 Christmas Charity Projects.

- *Angel Tree* is a ministry of Prison Fellowship, delivering love in the form of Christmas gifts and a message of hope to children of prisoners. Learn more about Angel Tree projects by going to http://www.angeltree.org.
- *Operation Christmas Child* invites you to pack a shoebox with small toys, school supplies, other gifts, and a personal note to be delivered to needy children overseas. For more information, go to http://www.samaritanspurse.org and click on Operation Christmas Child.
- *Make a Wish Foundation* helps a child's dream come true. Their unique holiday donation options will help grant the wishes of children with life-threatening medical conditions. For information, contact http://www.wish.org.
- *Toys for Tots:* Donate a new toy or give a donation to help Christmas become a little brighter for a needy child in your community. For more information, contact www.toysfortots.org.
- *My Two Front Teeth* offers a personalized online gift-giving experience to aid underprivileged children who are allowed to individually pick one holiday wish. The child's wish profile is entered into the online database where donors then choose an online sponsorship. Learn more at http://mytwofrontteeth.org.
- Anything that you can make, sometimes with only minimal skill, can be donated somewhere. For a marvelous site listing charity crafting links that need donated supplies and services, such as layette gowns to be used for premature babies, hats, mittens, quilts, or knitted and crocheted items, go to www.bevscountrycottage.com/charity-links.html.
- The Holiday Project's mission is to enrich the experience of the holidays by arranging visits to people confined to nursing homes, hospitals, and other institutions. Go to http://holiday-project.org for more information about the project.
- *Volunteers of America* is a 113-year-old human service organization that offers volunteer opportunities through thousands of programs. To access their website, go to www.voa.org.

- The U.S. Department of Housing and Urban Development has a website for each state with information on volunteering for nationwide organizations, such as Habitat for Humanity, American Red Cross, American Cancer Society, and Big Brothers Big Sisters. Go to www.hud.gov/local/index.cfm?state to locate your state page, and then click on *homeless* or *volunteer opportunities*.
- The U.S. Administration on Aging has a website called The Eldercare Locator that can help locate home and community-based services like transportation, meals, home care, and caregiver support services. Go to www.eldercare.gov to contact area Agencies on Aging for volunteer opportunities.
- Call your local city hall and see if there are any community service Christmas projects in your area that you could help with.
- Check the phone book for social services or human services agencies.
- Many communities have a volunteer center where service opportunities are paired with volunteers who are seeking opportunities to serve.
- Many newspapers sponsor a "volunteer corner" in one of the weekend papers. Also watch your newspaper for contact numbers for Sub for Santa, Toys for Tots, Angel Tree, and other organizations that need volunteers to help for a couple of days during the season.
- Check with local senior citizen centers, nursing homes, hospitals, homeless shelters, or family and children's resource centers.
- Contact your local PTA president. They are often aware of service opportunities that are available to help school-age children.

CHAPTER 10

Teach with Symbolism

The Lord frequently uses symbols to teach us the nature of our relationship to Him. Our understanding of the gospel is beautified by the abundant use of symbols throughout the scriptures. Because the plan of salvation centers on the Savior as the one through whom salvation comes, most of the basic symbols and representations are likenesses of Him and his atoning sacrifice.

In the Pearl of Great Price we read, "And behold, all things have their likeness, and all things are created and made to bear record of me, both things which are temporal, and things which are spiritual; things which are in the heaven above, and things which are on the earth, and things which are in the earth, and things which are under the earth, both above and beneath: all things bear record of me" (Moses 6:63).

The most well-known symbol was the Mosaic law, which was given to help the people understand and look forward to the coming of Christ, as explained by Nephi: "Behold, my soul delighteth in proving unto my people the truth of the coming of Christ; for, for this end hath the Law of Moses been given; and all things which have been given of God from the beginning of the world, unto man, are the typifying of him" (2 Nephi 11:4).

The Savior taught His precepts couched in parables and symbolisms, with the directive that "he who hath ears to hear, let him hear." Paul instructs us, "Now we have received, not of the spirit of the world, but the spirit which is of God; that we might know the things that are freely given to us of God. Which things also we speak, not in the words which man's wisdom teacheth, but which the Holy Ghost teacheth; comparing spiritual things with spiritual. But the natural man receiveth not the things of the spirit of God: for they are foolishness unto him: neither can he know them, because they are spiritually discerned" (1 Corinthians 2:12-14).

Once while sitting in the celestial room of the temple, I was contemplating some choices that I needed to make and praying for more faith to make them. As I was pondering, I happened to look at a beautiful bureau that I was seated next to. It was a nice-sized semicircle in shape, and the workmanship of the wood was stunning. I found myself looking at it with such awe. I tried to see around the front of the piece, but I couldn't because I was seated right next to it. The Spirit whispered to me a symbolic lesson—that my life was like this piece of furniture. My carpenter had built for me an eternal life that is stunningly beautiful, but all I could see was the portion closest to me because of where I was in that moment in time. My mortal eyes could not see the larger picture and could not see the end of it from the beginning. I needed to have patience and faith in Him—faith that the finished product of my life would reflect every carving and every nail that the Lord had used to construct it, every sanding that was necessary to remove imperfections and refine it, and the varnish to protect it and preserve it. I needed to trust my Father in Heaven, who knows how best to fashion me into the piece of furniture that will be of greatest use in His eternal household.

This lesson was personal and poignant. This otherwise ordinary piece of furniture had become a symbol, allowing me to learn a principle of truth that I could apply to my own understanding. I will remember the lesson every time I see a rounded bureau. Such is the power that symbols have in teaching us valuable principles.

USING THE SYMBOLS OF CHRISTMAS

As we struggle to understand the meaning of Christmas and the manner in which we celebrate truth, it is important for us to relate what we are doing to why we are doing it. By using symbols to teach correct principles, we establish a sense of purpose in our motives and in our actions as we celebrate. We are reminded of the principal of truth each time we see the symbol because it evokes powerful memories.

"Yea, let all thy thoughts be directed unto the Lord; yea, let the affections of thy heart be placed upon the Lord forever" (Alma 37:36). Symbols are a way of directing our thoughts back to the Lord.

Christmas provides us with extraordinary opportunities to surround ourselves with symbols of our beloved Immanuel, everything from the gifts that we give to the decorations that we hang. But they remind us of Him only if we think about their spiritual applications. Without the teaching, the discussion, and the application, our traditions will become unfocused and worldly. They may be fun, they may be beautiful, but they will not serve any spiritual purpose. A candle may evoke warm memories, but it can do so much more if used as a visual aid in a tender moment of instruction.

To expect us to remember the true meaning of Christmas without ever having to be reminded is to deny the influence that living in this mortal world has upon us—an influence that will continue to affect us as long as we draw breath. We must be taught the truth, and the use of symbols helps us to connect our beliefs with our behavior. Our family tradition of giving three wise gifts has provided us with a symbolic way to teach our children about the deeper meanings of Christmas and the reason we have great cause to rejoice in the birth of Jesus Christ.

THE BATTLE FOR CHRISTMAS

Christmas stands precariously upon a precipice. Nonbelievers of Jesus Christ loudly shout "foul" and perpetuate a game of "whose holiday is it anyway?" In recent years, there has been a move by many large retail stores to eliminate all references to words that refer to Christ or Christmas in both decorating and advertising, all in the name of being "sensitive" to those who might take offense. There has also been a trend to demand that all employees of many companies eliminate any reference to Christ by wishing people "Merry Christmas."

It really shouldn't be a surprise to those who believe we are living in the last days that Satan is waging a battle to suppress anything and everything that furthers the cause of righteousness. In the Book of mormon we read, "At that day shall [Satan] rage in the hearts of the children of men, and stir them up to anger against that which is good" (2 Nephi 28:20).

Evil is reaching epidemic proportions, but I doubt we ever imagined that Christ would be driven completely out of Christmas. Just ten years ago, a Gallup poll showed that 90 percent of Americans recognize (not necessarily celebrate) Christmas as the birthday of Jesus Christ. Now the minority is shouting so loudly that the squeaky wheel is getting the grease. Mosiah explained the tendency this way: "Now it is not common that the voice of the people desireth anything contrary to that which is right; but it is common for the lesser part of the people to desire that which is not right" (Mosiah 29:26).

This "lesser part of the people" contend that it is not politically correct to celebrate Christmas when there are those among us who do not believe in Christ. To counter this movement, and to save our beloved Christmas, we must fight for our right to believe in the Savior. But a word of caution: if we, as followers of Christ, do not like the way that we ourselves celebrate Christmas, how do we expect others to tolerate our beliefs, much less align themselves to them?

In response to the blatant effort to take Christ out of Christmas, many religious groups around the country have found the courage to come together to boycott businesses that participate in these anti-Christ efforts. Many retail stores have learned that the silent majority is no longer content to be silent, that they have decided to wage battle against those who would take away their religious freedom. In response, nearly one thousand lawyers have come together in the defense of exercising the right to say "Merry Christmas" and opposing efforts to censor Christmas.

But this is not the only battlefront on the war for Christmas. Other groups of Christians are opposing Christmas, with the proclamation that the holiday does not really belong to the Savior anyway. Their contention is that it began as a pagan holiday and continues to be so due to the materialistic and commercial way that most people in America celebrate it.

Some Christians refuse to use most of the symbols of Christmas with the accusation that they were adapted from pagan rituals. They claim that Christians have been deceived, that all symbols and icons of a prior celebration honoring pagan gods should have no place in a celebration of the birth of the Son of God. It is somehow thought to be wrong to celebrate Christmas because a believer could unintentionally worship a false God.

Thus Satan has secretly waged war against Christmas from all sides and hopes to have the advantage of prevailing culture to win his war. Understanding these issues will help us disarm the theories of those who would try to remove Christ from Christmas.

The prophet Howard W. Hunter has addressed the pre-Christian origins of paganism this way:

> Christmas has come down to us as a day of thanksgiving and rejoicing—a day of good cheer and goodwill to men. Although it has an earthly relation and significance, it is divine in content. The ancient Christian celebration has lived continuously through the centuries. . . . The evolution from a pagan holiday transformed into a Christian festival to the birth of Christ in men's lives is another form of maturity that comes to one who has been touched by the gospel of Jesus Christ.[1]

Christmas has just grown up and changed into something better. When the pagan culture of Northern Europe turned to the gospel of Christ, they "Christianized" their traditions and redirected them to Christ. He brought light into the world—a world filled with pagan gods—and He largely conquered unbelief. It was these transformed Christians who chose to breathe new meaning into their old pagan customs. God himself has used familiar symbols and structured them with new meanings. The Law of Moses was done away with upon the advent of the sacrifice and Atonement of the Savior. "Therefore those things which were of old time, which were under the law, in me are all fulfilled. Old things are done away, and all things have become new" (3 Nephi 12:46, 47).

Granted, there are many symbols in early Christianity that had pagan heritage. There were also converts to Christianity that likewise had dubious pagan backgrounds. But old evils can be done away, and all things can become new in Christ—even the evil fir tree and the pagan evergreen bough hung over the door!

There are good and bad elements inherent in all holidays. We must make righteous decisions about which symbols we want to use, and we have the gift of the Holy Ghost to help us make those decisions. Perhaps the original use of a symbol may not be as important as how Christians have transformed the symbol to worship God.

CAUTIONARY CLAUSE

I'm not nearly as worried about the pagan beginnings of holly and ivy as I am about the harmfulness of the book *The Night Before Christmas*.

I know I will probably make enemies in saying this, but when we strive for spiritual and meaningful feelings on Christmas Eve by reading the story of the Savior's birth, why would we want to send our children off to bed with their minds filled with visions of sugarplums, reindeer, and Santa Claus? I want them to ponder the birth of the Savior!

Another concern is Santa's visits to our ward parties. How do we answer the concerns from our little children who say that because Santa comes to church, he must be real? Do we really want to confuse them about what is true and what is not? They will be faced with enough doubt and opposition in their young lives without adding more to it. If families choose not to have Santa as part of their celebrations, they feel like they are going against all social norms already without feeling at odds with their ward family. We should support one another in *any* effort to make our celebrations more spiritual and reverent.

I have seen some excellent solutions to this problem. One is to have the bishopric put on robes and visit the children as three wise men, giving them a little bag of gold chocolate coins and a candy cane. Another solution is to make the program portion of the ward's Christmas party so spiritual that Santa will never be missed. One year, our Primary presidency prepared a beautiful slide show presentation to be given at our ward Christmas dinner. During a fall Primary activity, they took the children out into a field where they had assembled a stable, a manger, and animals. All the children were given costumes and posed in different positions as shepherds, angels, wise men, the innkeeper, townspeople, and Mary and Joseph. Costumes were rearranged and used again as they took pictures of various scenes where they enacted the story of the Savior's birth. With scriptures and beautiful music, the slide show turned out absolutely wonderful.

Many wards have a Bethlehem night with activities that celebrate the coming of the Savior, and this always seems to be an enjoyable activity. Ward activity leaders should be creative in selecting meaningful activities for members to participate in. A friend told me once that at her ward Christmas party, not one of the eight or so songs that were sung was of a spiritual nature. Wards and branches need to set the stage, so to speak, as examples.

However activity leaders choose to add more spirituality to their celebrations, I would suggest that they should start by tackling Santa at the door and telling him that he doesn't have a ticket, and that he is needed back at the mall immediately!

SYMBOLIC MEANINGS

Following is a list of symbols that have been used over the course of history to teach important truths of Christianity. When used effectively, symbols can help remind us of the reasons for the season, thus attaching importance and purpose to our celebrations. When such symbols are used, take time to explain them to your family.

Chrismons

Many of the symbols that we see associated with Christmas were used by Christians from the earliest days of their conversion. The word *Chrismon* is sometimes used to denote symbols of Christ and the Christian faith. The word *Chrismon* comes from a combination of "CHRISt's MONograms." One of the most well-known and most ancient Chrismons is the symbol of a fish, used in the early days of Christianity to reveal the identity of a follower of Jesus Christ.

Many Christians use Chrismons to decorate their Christmas tree as a way of centering their celebration on Christ. These icons or symbols are sometimes cut from white paper since the color white is considered the symbol for the Savior's purity.

- *Three Gifts:* Three gifts are used to resemble the gifts given to Christ from the wise men—gold, frankincense, and myrrh. They are used as ornaments, in fragrant candles, and soaps and herbs. Frankincense and myrrh can be purchased today to use as a decorative display in remembrance of the first Christmas gifts.
- *Christmas Tree:* The color of the evergreen ("ever green") tree, still vibrant in the dead of winter, can symbolize the eternal life Jesus Christ provides, which enables us to overcome death. The everlasting green color reminds us of the everlasting hope of mankind. The green needles on each branch pointing heavenward remind us that our thoughts should turn toward heaven.
- *Tree of Life:* Some members of the Church choose to use an evergreen to remind them of everlasting, eternal life symbolized in the tree of life. Some use colored bulbs to represent the fruit, and some use pure white ornaments. The lights signify that everlasting life comes from the Savior, the light of the world.
- *Tree of Jesse:* The tree of Jesse is a popular symbol used in many

Christian religions. Jesse was the father of David, from whose line God chose to bring forth both Mary and Joseph, and thus the Messiah. Isaiah 11:1 says, "There shall come forth a rod out of the stem of Jesse." In many Christian denominations, the Jesse Tree has become a tradition. Usually, it is decorated with ornaments that are associated with the Old Testament, such as a rainbow for Noah's Ark, music for David, a lamp (the word of God is a light on our path), an apple (Garden of Eden), and so forth. Often, the Jesse Tree is used to collect items of warmth for the poor or homeless. The tree can be decorated with hats, scarves, gloves, mittens, socks, or any small item of clothing.

- *Wreath:* Wreaths symbolize the eternal nature of love. As a circle, it is one continuous round of affection. The greenery symbolizes eternal life. Some people use the wreath as a reminder of the crown of thorns that Jesus wore when He died on the cross to show His eternal love for us.
- *The Color Red:* The color red, so prominent everywhere at this season, is symbolic of the atoning sacrifice of Jesus Christ, as His blood was shed for all people that they might have the gifts of salvation and exaltation. Red is a deep color. It is considered the strongest color and is appropriate for God's gift of His son.
- *The Color Green:* The color green symbolizes that, according to modern revelation, Christ was not born in December, but in the springtime of the year, when life is renewed.
- *Lights:* The most enduring symbol of Christmas is that of lights, which are symbolic of declarations in the scriptures that Jesus Christ is the light and the life of the world. Christmas lights remind us of the great signs of light in the heavens as we see them on city streets and homes. To some, colorful bulbs symbolize the fruits of the tree of life.
- *Candles:* Candles can be used to symbolize many things. Some use candles to symbolize the star. Others use candles to symbolize Christ as the light of the world. Those who follow him "shall not walk in darkness, but shall have the light of life" (John 8:12). Others use candles to teach the Sermon on the Mount: "Neither do men light a candle, and put it under a bushel, but on a candlestick; and it giveth light unto all that are

in the house. Let your light so shine before men, that they may see your good works, and glorify your Father who is in heaven" (Matthew 5:15–16). When Joseph and Mary presented Jesus in the temple, Simon referred to the Christ child as "a light to lighten the Gentiles."

The lighting of candles has been a part of religious worship for centuries. The Hebrews burned candles for eight days as a part of the Festival of Lights, instituted by Judas Maccabeus in 165 BC to celebrate the purification of the temple of Jerusalem. This is now called Hanukkah.

- *Star:* The star on top of the Christmas tree symbolizes the new star that appeared in the heavens with the advent of the Savior to guide the wise men and the shepherds to the stable. It was a heavenly sign of prophecy fulfilled with the shining hope of all mankind. The star is also symbolic of Jesus, who is often called the "bright and morning star."
- *Angels:* Sometimes shown as blowing a trumpet, these are God's messengers sent to proclaim the good news to Mary, the shepherds, the wise men, and the world. It also represents the angels who rejoiced with singing from the heavens.
- *Bells:* Bells ring out to guide lost sheep back to the fold, so it should ring out for people everywhere to return to the fold.
- *Carols:* Christmas carols, sung only at Christmastime, remind us of the multitude of the heavenly hosts who sang "Glory to God in the highest, and on earth peace, goodwill toward men."
- *Gifts:* Gifts remind us that Jesus was the best gift that God could ever give to us. The wise men gave gifts to infant Jesus, and we should likewise remember to give real gifts of love at Christmas.
- *Bows:* The bow can be a symbol that all men should be tied together with the bonds of goodwill toward each other. As the bow is untied, we can be reminded to have love and good feelings toward each other.
- *Candy Canes:* There are many stories told about the origin of the candy cane, but it probably doesn't matter where it comes from as much as the principle of truth that it is used to symbolize. Candy canes usually symbolize a shepherd's crook, used to

bring back the strayed sheep to the fold. It can remind us that we are our brother's keeper. It also can represent the staff of the Good Shepherd to reach all the fallen lambs, who, like sheep, have gone astray.

Some use a deeper symbolism for the candy cane. The white color is said to symbolize the virgin birth and sinless nature of Christ. The stripes represent the stripes Jesus received when He was beaten before His crucifixion; the large red stripe is for the blood shed by Christ on the cross. The cane is in the form of a "J" to represent the precious name of Jesus.

- *Advent Wreaths:* Christians have long made and used advent wreaths from evergreens that symbolize eternal life. A circle with no beginning or end, it represents eternal life. There are traditionally four candles around the wreath with an additional candle in the center. The meaning and the colors of the candles differ from church to church, but most commonly there are three purple candles that many Christians use to represent hope, peace, and love. The fourth candle is rose or red, and represents new life gained through Christ's sacrifice. The first Sunday following Thanksgiving, one purple candle is lit during a devotional. The second Sunday, two purple candles are lit, on the third two purple and one rose, and finally all four on the last week of Advent. The light from the candles signifies the light of Christ, growing brighter as He comes into the world. Most often, a white candle is used in the center to represent Christ's birth and is lit on Christmas Eve. Even though as a church we do not recognize Advent, assigning a specific meaning to each candle could customize this tradition to represent values taught during family home evening.

- *Holly and Ivy:* Because the holly puts forth bright red berries in the dead of winter, it has been considered a symbol of endless life. In addition, the sharpness of the bush and the redness of the berries have associated with the crown of thorns Christ wore and the blood He shed for us with His crucifixion. The Danish have called this bush the "Christ thorn." For generations, Christians have placed holly in their windows as a sign that Christ has entered their homes.

Ivy has been used extensively for Christmas decorating since the Middle Ages. It was considered a symbol of love because of its clinging habit of growth, and of everlasting love and life, because it is an evergreen.
- *Fruit:* The tree of life described in the book of Revelation has twelve different kinds of fruit. This is part of the traditional tree decorations in some parts of Europe, where they hang real fruit on the evergreen tree and eat from it through the holiday season. Fruit of the tree of life of course represents eternal life as the greatest of God's gifts to man (see 1 Nephi 8).

Other symbols that can be used to teach important truths:
- *Alpha and Omega:* The first and the last letters of the Greek alphabet symbolize that Christ is the beginning and the end.
- *Lamb:* Represents our Lord Jesus as the sacrificial lamb for all our sins. Nativity scenes frequently show a pure white lamb closest to the Christ child to remind us that he is pure and an innocent lamb of God who was sent to be sacrificed for the sins of the world.
- *Shepherd:* Christ is the Good Shepherd, and shepherds rejoiced at His coming.
- *Bread:* Bethlehem, where He was born, means "house of bread." This most common food was chosen by the Savior Himself as a remembrance of his life: "I am the living bread."
- *Nail:* Hung with a crimson bow, a nail can become a symbol of His nail-pierced hands and the blood He shed for us.
- *Keys:* Symbolize the keys of the kingdom of heaven (Matthew 16:19).
- *Donkey:* Symbolizes the animals in the stable.
- *Song:* A symbol to remember to sing the praises of the Lord as did the angels.
- *Crown:* Symbolizes that Christ is the King of Kings.
- *Sword:* Represents truth.
- *Trumpet:* Represents the ushering in of the last days.
- *Heart:* Symbolizes the love in our hearts for others.
- *Dove:* A representation and symbol of the Holy Ghost.
- *Church:* Reminds us that the people of God come together to worship Him.

LEGENDS

Legends are stories handed down from generation to generation that are presented as history but are unlikely to be true. The following legends do not have known authors, and there are many variations that can be found with a little research. I have included two legends from the sea that are often used to decorate Christmas trees—the starfish and the sand dollar.

The legend of the nutcracker is a favorite story of German children, and if used to teach selflessness and a change of heart, the nutcracker can be a valuable symbol. Legends of symbols are stories that impart meaning and reason to the symbol, and they tend to be passed down because of their ability to teach.

The Legend of the Nutcracker

Beneath the wooden exterior of the handsomely carved nutcracker lies a rich heritage that comes from the Erzgebirge (Ore Mountains) of Germany, where the legend is told even today.

> There once was a rich farmer, who was very miserly and lonely. His heart was as hard as the walnuts he grew on his many properties, but he had no time to crack them to get the tasty meat inside. So he offered a reward to anyone who could find an easy way to crack the nuts. Many unusual ideas were proposed but none were accepted by him. Then one day an old puppet carver came to him with a beautiful puppet painted to look like a local miner in dress uniform, with a large mouth and a strong jaw. The jaws were strong enough to crack the hard walnuts.
>
> The miserly farmer was delighted by that and decided to reward the whole village. After then, every year at Christmastime, he gave all the village people fruitcake, and chocolates with nuts. He even had some walnuts painted gold to be the decorations on the Christmas tree. He gave the puppet carver a special workshop so that he was free to make the most beautiful nutcrackers in the world. So not only did the beautiful nutcracker crack the walnuts, he also cracked open the heart of the farmer so that he was open to kindness and generosity.[2]

Legend of the Christmas Tree

Legend has it that Martin Luther was the first to decorate his home with a Christmas tree over four centuries ago. He was walking home on

Christmas Eve when he saw the stars shining upon the snow-covered branches of fir trees. He was so taken by the sight that he took a tree home and placed candles on the branches to demonstrate to his family what a glorious sight he had seen. From this first Christmas tree in the Luther household, the German people began using a Christmas tree in their homes.

Legend of the Christmas Stocking

Through the centuries, many legends and stories have been told about the life and deeds of Saint Nicholas, the Bishop of Myra. One popular account tells of a peasant who lived happily in a small cottage with his wife and three daughters. One day, the wife suddenly died of an illness, leaving the man and his three daughters in despair. When the daughters reached a marriageable age, the poor father became even more depressed, for he knew he could in no way marry them off to good men without a dowry.

St. Nicholas had come to know of the peasant and his daughters, and he wanted to do something secretly to help them. He went to the peasant's house one night with a bag of gold and waited for the family to go to bed so he could throw the bag through the open window.

That night, after finishing their washing for the day, the daughters had hung their stockings by the fireside to dry, and St. Nicholas tiptoed to the cottage and peeked in. He saw the stockings and carefully put the gold in one of them. When the father found the bag the next morning, he was ecstatic because now he would have a dowry for one of his daughters.

A second time, St. Nicholas came and once again put gold in one of the stockings, this time enough to allow the second daughter to be married. But by now the father had become eager to find out who the kind benefactor was, so when St. Nicholas tried a third time to place gold in one of the stockings, the man recognized him and cried out in joy and gratitude and thanked him with all his heart. He was able to see all three of his daughters married, and lived a long and happy life thereafter.

Legend of the Starfish

A vacationing businessman was walking along a beach when he saw a young boy. Along the shore were many starfish that had been washed up by the tide and were sure to die before the tide returned.

The boy walked slowly along the shore and occasionally reached down and tossed a beached starfish back into the ocean. The businessman, hoping to teach the boy a little lesson in common sense, walked up to the boy and said, "I have been watching what you are doing, son. You have a good heart, and I know you mean well, but do you realize how many beaches there are around here and how many starfish are dying on every beach every day? Surely such an industrious and kindhearted boy like yourself could find something better to do with your time. Do you really think that what you are doing is going to make a difference?" The boy looked up at the man, and then he looked down at a starfish by his feet. He picked up the starfish, and as he gently tossed it back into the ocean, he said, "It makes a difference to that one."

The Legend of the Sand Dollar

The Legend of the Sand Dollar is an Easter and Christmas favorite. It tells a story that includes the five slits representing the wounds on Christ when on the cross and the Easter lily with a star in the middle representing the star of Bethlehem. On the back is the outline of a poinsettia, the Christmas flower. The Legend of the Sand Dollar also tells of the five doves that are inside and how the sand dollar spreads good will and peace when it is broken open.

> Upon this odd-shaped seashell a legend grand is told,
> About the life of Jesus, the wondrous tale of old.
> At its center you will see, there seems to be a star,
> Like the one that led the shepherds and wise men from afar.
> Around its surface are the marks of nails and thorns and spear,
> Suffered by Christ upon the cross; the wounds show plainly here.
> But there is also an Easter lily, clear for us to see,
> The symbol of Christ's resurrection for all eternity.[3]

Notes

1. Elder Howard W. Hunter, *The Real Christmas* (Salt Lake City: Bookcraft, 1993), 3, 6.
2. For a version of this legend, see "Exploring: Cracking Nuts," *Friend*, Dec. 1984, 35.
3. There are several versions of this poem, often found on postcards, greeting cards, plaques, and gift store items. However, the author and original publication date are unknown.

IDEAS ON USING
SYMBOLS
TO TEACH

- When giving treats to neighbors and friends, relate them to a spiritual theme, and make a decorative tag relating a scripture, etc. For instance:
    - "An *angel* brought the glorious news that a Savior had been born."
    - "Wise men and shepherds followed a bright *star* to the manger where Jesus lay."
    - "Let the *bells* ring out this holiday season as we celebrate Jesus' birthday and God's greatest gift to us.

    Some dear neighbors of mine have perfected the practice of giving thoughtful gifts that have spiritual meaning. They always include a message to relate the symbol to the gift. For instance, one year they gave homemade soap with following message: "As you use these handmade soaps which have been scented with frankincense and myrrh, we hope that you remember not only the gifts that the wise men shared with the baby Jesus, but also the many precious gifts that the Savior has given to each of us. May this Christmas season bring you joy and happiness as you continue to serve and to follow the teachings of our Savior, Jesus Christ."
- Make Christmas sugar cookies and cut them out into shapes as symbols to represent certain aspects of why we celebrate the season. If desired, cut out shapes to represent the Nativity scene. Watch for cookie cutters in shapes that can be used as symbols to teach children while they enjoy the process.
- Have a family home evening to explain the use of common symbols of Christmas. Throughout the holidays, use additional teaching moments by relating the symbols to the true reason for the season.
- Some people give neighborhood gifts with little sayings and

rhymes. Although creative, reindeer poop (Milk Duds) really has nothing to do with Christmas. Instead, use gifts that have symbolism and meaning. For example, a new ornament for a Christmas tree to represent an aspect of the first Christmas will not only be cherished for its simplicity but also the beautiful way in which it conveys the need to center all things on the Savior.

- Your family may choose to use the decorations on your Christmas tree as symbols. Using Matthew 7:16–18, teach that a good tree brings forth good fruits. Fruit ornaments can be used to represent good acts that you have accomplished individually or as a family, such as service projects or kindnesses shown to one another.
- You may want a particular color of ornament to reflect the time you have spent reading the scriptures or having family devotions where the Savior is the topic of your conversation. Some families use the lights of the tree to reflect these things, adding more lights as the season progresses.
- Center your Christmas tree decorations around a symbol that the family has chosen to highlight for the year. For instance, have a theme of bells, angels, shepherds, or any other favorite symbol. You may want to have a "CTR" tree for Primary-aged children by using glitter paint to write CTR on glass balls.
- When choosing traditions for your family, use symbols to explain them. For instance, some families have a tradition of baking a birthday cake for Jesus. A round cake is symbolic that there is no end—He is the alpha and the omega. Use white icing to represent His purity and red candles for His atoning sacrifice. The light of the candles represents the light of Christ. A star could be used in the center to remind us of the star of Bethlehem, or an angel sitting on top of the cake would remind us that the angels sang for joy.
- Play Symbol Bingo. Make bingo cards with pictures of Christmas symbols on them. Use stickers or clip art, or have children draw pictures on the cards. Make word strips that describe the symbol. Place in a bowl and pull out one by one. Use Christmas candy as markers. The first one to get bingo gets to eat the candy. Or for older children, use a scriptural reference for that symbol. After hearing the reference, children look up the scripture and the first one to get the name of the symbol is the only one who can claim it on his card.

CHAPTER 11

Enjoy Quality Traditions

The movie *Fiddler on the Roof* has always been a favorite of mine. I can scarcely hear the word *tradition* without thinking of Tevye and life in Anatevka. "Because of our tradition, every one of us knows who he is and what God expects him to do," declares Tevye. "Traditions! Traditions! Traditions! Without our traditions our lives would be as shaky as a fiddler on the roof!"

Traditions weave their way through life in every corner of the world. Some have existed so long that we have forgotten their original purpose, and there are some we have only recently developed to meet our current needs. They range in size from small to large, but even the simplest of traditions can be important. Sometimes referred to as rituals, they offer children a sense of structure and security, family closeness, and moral values. They can be quirky little things that we do as families, which children tend to hold onto tightly.

Holidays become memorable to our family members because of the uniqueness of our individual traditions and how they shape our family histories. Think about how often family members talk about good times and good memories that happened as they were carrying out some tradition or another. Traditions are at the heart of nearly every family gathering or celebration. They give us comfort and reassurance that we have a special place in our family.

THE HUMBLE BEGINNINGS OF TRADITIONS

Sometimes we create traditions without even realizing it. One year I took our kids up the canyon to play in the leaves and to take some fun fall pictures during an October school break. We enjoyed it so much that we've repeated it every year. Another time, when our daughter was just three years old, I kissed her good night on her forehead. As I was leaving the room, she called me back and told me, "You didn't do it right!" When I asked her what she meant, she said, "Mommy, don't you know? It's a tradition! You kiss me three times right here." She pointed to her cheek.

Even the smallest rituals have an impact. They are the things that children look forward to and miss if they don't happen. They are actions that speak louder than words, and usually come from the things that you and your children love to do.

There are ethnic traditions that have been part of family celebrations for years. For instance, a friend of mine gets together with her extended family on Christmas Eve and makes homemade tamales. These types of traditions are important because they give continuity and a unique flavor to our celebrations, and these are the ones that we should probably consider carefully before changing.

When couples first marry, the process of bringing two people together to start a new family usually means that there are now two different views on how to celebrate Christmas. They must develop new ways to look at the holiday together. To help achieve that, couples should ask themselves, "What traditions do we want with our immediate family, and what do we want with our extended family?" Both husband and wife should choose their most important expectation and then brainstorm about how best to achieve both of them.

In my home, it was my father who had the greatest delight in decorating our tree and home, but in my husband's family, his mother was the one who had that privilege. Naturally, after we were married, there was some disagreement as to who should decorate our tree. So we compromised. Dad has to get out all the decorations (and put them away later). And while we decorate the tree, he has to visit with us while we drink eggnog and listen to Christmas music together.

There are as many different types of traditions as there are individual families, and so we need to tailor them to fit our particular circumstances. Most of us have some things in common—almost every family sets up a Christmas tree and stockings, and usually has some traditional American food to eat, such as turkey or ham. There are also traditions that have become Latter-day Saint favorites, which include caroling as a family, baking cookies, reading and acting out the story of the Savior's birth, and receiving new pajamas on Christmas Eve. There are a couple of traditions that surface often, one of which is the custom of placing a piece of straw on the manger for every act of kindness and having a special way of giving a gift to the Savior.

TEACHING WITH TRADITIONS

Some traditions come about as teaching moments, such as our family's tradition of being our children's first date after they turn sixteen. Sons had a date to look forward to with Mom, and daughters went with Dad. It gave us time to reinforce valuable lessons about treating others with respect and honor. Another teaching moment turned into a tradition when I gave my youngest daughter a bouquet of yellow daffodils for Easter with a note explaining that the color yellow is symbolic of the brightest element in the sky—the sun (the Son of God), reminding us to always look to the Creator of all life and growth.

If a family finds that a particular practice makes them feel closer to the Savior and to each other, they will probably decide to repeat it the following year. If it continues to bring joy and satisfaction to the family, it may become a cherished tradition that is handed down from generation to generation.

The traditions that we observe strengthen our family ties, binding us to the past, present, and future. They help us define our own identities but still have the power to give us continuity and security, especially those traditions that express our fondness and affection for each other.

Traditions have great potential to show children what parents value the most, and they are a vital way to convey spiritual conviction. Children will believe that whatever is repeated regularly has significance to us. Much of the spiritual learning and the building of our testimonies come from the feeling and reverence that we exercise by virtue of our traditions.

CHOOSING QUALITY TRADITIONS

Any tradition that takes a lot of time should be evaluated in terms of whether or not it brings us closer to Christ. We should ask ourselves the following six questions:

1. Which traditions give me the greatest joy?
2. Do we enjoy the tradition, or do we continue it because we think it's expected?
3. Are the benefits worth the time, energy, and money expended?
4. Is there someone who could help with this tradition so that it's not a burden?
5. If we decide to eliminate this tradition, how will others feel about it?
6. If all my traditions involve other people, is there a tradition that I could begin to enhance my own feelings of joy?

Some traditions are so beneficial that we would never think of changing them. However, some traditions can and should be adapted as the needs of our family change. Use what works best for your situation, but don't feel the need to continue traditions that no longer work for you. Traditions shouldn't destroy the very relationships that they are trying to build.

Sometimes people believe that if we repeat any activity, we are destined to keep it forever. They say, "But it's a tradition!" Our family has six basic traditions, and those six traditions are the ones that are so sacred to us that we choose to repeat them year after year (I'm sure you'll recognize them):

1. We simplify our gift giving.
2. We give gifts all year. This also includes gifts of service.
3. We choose meaningful activities to give us positive family experiences.
4. We serve others.
5. We teach with symbolism to enhance spiritual understanding.
6. We have fun tailoring quality traditions to meet our needs.

To illustrate, we know that we want to have the tradition of serving others, as this is paramount to having the spirit during the Christmas season. But we try to be flexible in choosing which service to perform each year, based on our family's needs. We believe that the more acts of service that children become involved with, the broader the scope of positive experiences they will have, as compared with doing the same Sub-for-Santa project year after year. Things sometimes need to be mixed up a bit to keep us from becoming desensitized by repetitiveness.

Uplifting traditions play a significant role in leading us toward things of the Spirit. Of necessity, we must cultivate traditions in our families that set standards for how we behave and how we show our dedication to the Lord. We should especially embrace those traditions of righteousness that enable us to grow spiritually and discard all those that create a barrier to our eternal view. Our traditions should promote love for Deity and unity in our families.

The tradition of righteousness sets a pattern for life, a legacy for our children, and brings us closer to God. And of course, the greatest tradition of all is also the very reason we celebrate Christmas: It is our love of Jesus Christ, and all our other traditions should point us in His direction as we seek after Him, follow Him, and try to become like Him.

IDEAS FOR FUN
Traditions

NEIGHBORHOOD TRADITIONS

- Host a neighborhood Christmas concert for everyone on your street. This could involve families, who choose what they would like to present together, or it could be just for children. Presentations could be musical numbers, a story or other type of performance, or other such talents. Deliver invitations and ask each family to bring some Christmas goodies to share.
- Hold a neighborhood Christmas caroling party. You could hold a group sing-along at someone's home, or go to other homes to carol. Everyone brings a plate of goodies to share.
- Have a live Nativity for the neighborhood. Schedule the presentation for a specific time, and use all the children from the neighborhood. Invite parents, friends, and neighbors. Serve Christmas cookies and hot chocolate or wassail as refreshments.
- Organize a Christmas play with the children in the neighborhood. Children can help by making the backdrops and costumes. Have them present it to the parents, at the ward Christmas party, or to the local nursing home. Or organize it to present during Boxing Day, the day after Christmas. In Britain, it is customary to put on plays on that day.
- Have a cookie-baking party with the children in the neighborhood. Have lots of cookie dough, frosting, and decorations on hand, and let the children make cookies to take home to their families.
- Create a neighborhood store for young children. Collect small gifts from the parents (something they have around the house or from the dollar store) and put together into a store, give children Christmas money and allow the children to purchase a new gift for their parents.

- Instead of exchanging presents with neighbors, use the money that would have been spent on each other and have a food drive for the local food bank. Afterward, have a get-together with a plate of treats from each family.
- Have a snowman-making contest with the neighborhood kids.
- Conduct a talent show. Invite anyone who is interested—adults or children—to share their talents. Present the talent show to parents, senior centers, homebound individuals, or anyone who would enjoy this kind of cheering up.

SEASONAL TRADITIONS

- Welcome visitors to your home with a Christmas message. Bake gingerbread men or sugar cookies, or purchase wrapped candies. Wrap the treats in a small square of fabric along with a written scriptural Christmas message and tie it with a ribbon. Keep these in a basket by the door to give out.
- Begin using your family's nice Christmas dishes on the first day of December. Use them every evening until the Christmas holidays are over.
- Have a special tablecloth that is used just for family celebrations each year. When you get together, have everyone sign his or her name on the cloth so that it can be viewed the next year.
- Read the scriptures or Christmas stories by candlelight all month, while having a snack.
- Sew a new Christmas pillowcase for each of the children or grandchildren to use during the month of December.
- After presents are opened on Christmas morning, have a wrapping paper fight.
- Have a snowball fight together as a family. Afterward, go into the house and have hot cocoa and eat snowballs made from ice cream that has been shaped into balls and rolled in coconut. Make the ice cream snowballs beforehand and put them in the freezer to set while you play outside.
- Invite another family to go with you to the mountains for a sledding and tubing party. Take hot chocolate, soup, or chili in a thermos and enjoy the splendors of playing in the snow.
- Take a Christmas stroll. Many people enjoy doing this on Christmas Day.

- Make hot chocolate from scratch. Then put on coats and mittens and go outside to sip the cocoa in the cool winter air.
- Have a fireworks display on Christmas Eve, or give children sparklers to use in the snow. Most city ordinances allow for the use of fireworks three days before and three days after Independence Day, Chinese New Year, New Year's Eve, and Christmas. Check your local ordinances to make sure fireworks are allowed. If so, they are a fun way to celebrate the importance of the holiday.
- Roast marshmallows over a fire in the fireplace, or be daring enough to try roasting chestnuts.
- String popcorn or cranberries together to decorate the tree. This would be a fun activity to do while watching a favorite Christmas movie.
- After decorating the house and the tree, sit on a blanket in the living room and have a tree picnic. The menu can vary from pizza to sandwiches or finger foods. Listen to beautiful music together or watch a favorite movie.
- Allow children to camp out under the lights of the Christmas tree. Have lots of snacks to munch on, and leave the lights on all night.
- Begin a family jigsaw puzzle on the first day of Christmas break or on Christmas Day and see if you can finish it by New Year's Day. Try to locate one that is made from a Nativity scene or another meaningful Christmas theme.
- Collect costumes and props such as a baby doll and a stuffed lamb for children to play with as Nativity dress-ups during the season.
- If your missionary is serving in a foreign country, read up on that country's Christmas traditions; then try them out at home.
- Have a family heritage Christmas. If your ancestors are from France, choose French Christmas foods and traditions. Learn to say Merry Christmas in French. Then next year, use traditions from another country of your family heritage.
- Host a genealogy dinner. Invite guests to bring a potluck dish from a country that reflects their own family heritage. If desired, have guests research and share some Christmas traditions from their chosen country.
- Have children make Christmas cards for friends, teachers, or cousins. These can be made from old cards, or have children draw their own illustrations. For extra quality, take the picture to the local print shop to turn it into a greeting card.

- Write a family Christmas letter, and allow each member of the family to write their own section. In this way, the communication will seem more natural, personal, and based in reality. (Some families prefer to write a spiritual note or another personal communication in their Christmas cards instead of a family Christmas letter.)
- Put together a family history for the year in the form of a newspaper. Cover the highlights of the family for the year. Have children help write it and assemble it. Or update your family's Christmas scrapbook for a memorable keepsake.
- Hang photos of your family members, both living and deceased, on your Christmas tree.
- Take a family portrait during the week of Christmas, and then include the picture in a newsletter sent on New Year's. Use the sofa as a way to have three levels (floor, sofa, standing). Hold a fun sign that shows the family name and the year.
- Take a family photo around the Christmas tree each year. This way there is a record of each year's tree as well as each child's growth from year to year. Or take a family photo on New Year's Eve. Everyone could wear clothing that represents an activity from the past year, such as a cheerleading outfit.
- Take a picture of each child every year on the same day, such as at midnight on New Year's Eve. This kind of activity is family history in the making.
- Teach children to appreciate other religions. For example, understand what Hanukkah is by playing a game of dreidel and eating latkes while watching the movie *Miracle at Moreaux*, a Christmas movie in which Jewish and Christian children come together and develop appreciation for each other and for the season.
- Give the animals around your home a Christmas present. Dip pine cones in peanut butter and seeds and hang onto the trees outside as a treat for birds.
- Plant a pine tree or fir tree in the yard that children can have fun decorating each year. Use popcorn or cranberry garlands, fruit, and other natural edibles for the birds.
- Have a grandparents' party. Invite your grandkids but not their parents. Provide some fun activities to do with your grandchildren, and have a fun time together. You may choose to give them new pajamas and have a pajama fashion show, followed by a sleepover.

- Plan a "mystery night" where the whole family gets together for an activity, but only Mom knows what the activity will be for the evening.
- Hold an audio scavenger hunt with a group of friends or as an extended family activity. Dividing into groups and using a tape recorder, each group goes to neighbors' homes and must record certain things, such as someone singing a song, telling a Christmas poem, ringing a bell, and so on. Be creative in coming up with ideas together.
- Make it a tradition to have a cousin get-together. Rotate the home every year and have potluck or make it a "just dessert affair." Or for even more ease, agree to meet at a local restaurant and have some laughs together.
- Have a tradition in which all the women in the extended family meet at a restaurant for lunch the day after Christmas to relax and take some much-deserved rest from the chores.
- Allow time for the boys and the men of the family to enjoy being together while doing something that is meaningful to them, such as skiing or snowmobiling. The girls and the women can get together at another time to go skiing while the dads hold down the fort, or they can enjoy other favorite activities such as going to a movie or scrapbooking together.
- Hold a stocking exchange between grown sisters, since moms don't usually get a stocking. Have a potluck party, rotating houses every year. Exchange stockings that have been filled with presents that fit pre-determined rules, such as that all gifts must cost less than five dollars.
- Celebrate the old German tradition of the pickle ornament. Custom has it that it should be the last ornament hung on the tree, hidden from view in the branches of the tree. On Christmas morning, the first child to find the ornament is the first to unwrap his or her gifts and receives an extra gift.
- Make each child a new handmade ornament and present it on Christmas Eve.
- Make the ornaments on your tree part of your family history. Purchase a new ornament each year while visiting a new destination or experiencing a memorable family event, such as the birth of a baby or a wedding

- Present each child with a new ornament that represents something they have accomplished during the year or something they have developed an interest in. Or have children pick out their own ornament each year. If desired, engrave it with the year and the child's name. These are kept in a special box and the child gets to hang these ornaments on the tree every year. When the child leaves home, the ornaments go with them.
- Make Christmas ornaments with your child's latest photo portrait. Write the date on the ornament and collect them through the years. Some families decorate the trees using only family photos.
- Clothing often plays a part in family celebrations. Some families get new pajamas on Christmas Eve every year. Christmas slippers, shirts, sweaters, and sweatshirts also play a part in family traditions.
- Some families put the craziest pair of socks that they can find into their children's stockings each year. For added fun, everyone puts on their crazy socks and then a picture is taken of their feet.
- Proclaim a family pajama day. Everyone stays in their pajamas and watches movies, plays board games, reads stories, and has breakfast foods for dinner.
- Make or buy a small stocking to use, filling it with candy or a personal note. Give it to another family member in secret, and that person then fills the stocking and passes it on to another family member.
- Many families with Spanish ancestry participate in Las Posadas ("the inns"), which is a nine-day celebration that is a yearly tradition for many Mexicans and other Latin Americans. It symbolizes the trials that Mary and Joseph endured before finding a place to stay where Jesus could be born. Typically, each family in a neighborhood will schedule a night for the Posada to be held at their home, starting on the 16th of December and finishing on the 24th. The hosts of the Posada act as the innkeepers, and the neighborhood children and adults are the pilgrims who have to request lodging by going house to house and singing a traditional song about Joseph and Mary.
- Have a Mexican-themed Christmas party with a piñata and a meal of enchiladas or tamales.

- Families with Swedish ancestry often celebrate with the appearance of St. Lucia. She is dressed in a long white dress and wears a crown of evergreen leaves topped by seven lighted candles. She leads a procession of girls and their mothers all dressed in long white dresses and each carrying a lighted candle. The purity symbolized by the white dresses makes this tradition a unique and endearing one. Depending on your locality, you may be able to find a local Santa Lucia festival.
- Eat a customary Chinese dinner with fish. According to Chinese tradition, eating fish will bring good fortune.
- If you have Danish ancestry, try a traditional Danish rice pudding, ris alamonde, which has an almond hidden inside. When eaten, the person must hide the almond in his or her mouth while everyone tries to guess who has the almond. That person then receives a prize.
- Conduct family interviews on Christmas Eve or New Year's Eve. Each person is interviewed and videotaped while seated in a special place and answers questions regarding his favorite things, interests, accomplishments of the year, goals, and so forth. You may choose to add other things to your video, such as a song or funny story. Each child is interviewed each year. Compile the interviews and make them into a slide presentation or movie to watch the next year.
- Have a tree farewell party on New Year's Day. Have a picnic party in front of the tree and then take the decorations down while reminiscing about the season.
- Have a pinecone burning ceremony. These are symbolic because of their nature to open up and bear fruit. Each person tosses a pine cone into the fire as they mention one way that they hope to "bear fruit" in the coming year.
- Include a nice set of thank-you cards in each child's stocking. Then, on the last day in December, the family writes the notes to extended family members and relatives.
- Develop a kiss that is unique to your family—a "trademark"—such as one long and then two short kisses on the forehead. Or invent a silent symbol of your family's love, such as a thumbs-up or a tug of an earlobe. Use it often to spread some of that Christmas spirit around all year.

CHAPTER 12

Guide Us to Thy Perfect Light

I began my journey to Bethlehem many years ago. As I made my way through rocky hillsides, I found lessons to be learned at every turn of the trail. I might not have steered clear of every rock or boulder that blocked my path, but in the end, the star shone brightly to light my way.

As a seeker of the light, I needed that wondrous star to point me to Christ. Its bright rays illuminated things that were obscured before by the approaching darkness. The adversary delights when he can deceive us gradually, obscuring light in degrees so indiscernible that that we are not even aware of the imminent darkness. Gradually, imperceptibly, we are enticed into the ways of the world, unaware of the mounting pressure and influence around us. This is the way that materialism, consumerism, and unparalleled busyness have crept into our Christmas unseen.

It shouldn't be difficult for us to remember the fundamental purpose of Christmas. It seems so simple and straightforward, but many of us still continue to struggle. Neal A. Maxwell made this observation about those who fail to leave room in their hearts for Christ: "They are *busy* and may not be in transgression, but they are certainly in *diversion*."[1]

Satan desires to divert us, and he will use whatever tactics he can to persuade us to change our direction if he thinks we are headed on the right course. Diversion makes it difficult to keep focused on that which is essential during the Christmas season, which is to remain focused first upon our Savior.

Every Christian who celebrates Christmas should ask himself these probing questions: "What diversions are keeping me from putting Christ back into Christmas? Has the devotion and love of the Lord tempered the demands of my time as far as Christmas is concerned? Would the Lord be happy with the way I have celebrated His birth?" These are the questions I found the courage to ask myself along my journey as I was prompted to search the skies above for a light to fill my soul.

It was so appropriate that the Lord would use a symbol of light to show us the way. The light from that majestic star came in the meridian of time, as if it were God's own finger pointing the way to Christ. The light was symbolic to proclaim the coming of His beloved Son into the world, as Jesus Christ would soon become the Light of the World.

To the new world, the sign of the coming of the Lord to the Nephites and Lamanites was, "One day and a night and a day, as if it were one day and there were no night" (Helaman 14:4). This was not just a random show of power from above. It was also a symbolic proclamation to the world that Christ had indeed come.

Ultimately, it is the light of Christ that shines brightly into the souls of men and directs them back into the presence of the Father. "Behold, I am the light which shineth in darkness. . . . Behold, I am Jesus Christ, the Son of God. I am the life and the light of the world" (D&C 11:11, 28).

The Savior's light grows stronger and brighter anytime we commemorate His birth, His life, or His sacrifice. It is the affirmation of the Holy Ghost. "For by my Spirit will I enlighten them, and by my power will I make known unto them the secrets of my will—yea, even those things which eye has not seen, nor ear heard, nor yet entered into the heart of man" (D&C 76: 10).

I have been a witness to the truth that God will reveal the secrets of His will through the gift of the Holy Ghost as He helps us along the way during this mortal journey. We are not left alone. He has promised us that, and we have been blessed with the Comforter, which will be with us always if we will but listen to the stillness. What a glorious gift is the Holy Ghost!

Developing the skill of listening to the Holy Ghost is so vital that following his martyrdom, the Prophet Joseph appeared to President

Brigham Young and said of the Spirit, "Tell the people to be humble and faithful, and be sure to keep the Spirit of the Lord and it will lead them right. Be careful and not turn away the small still voice; it will teach you what to do and where to go; it will yield the fruits of the kingdom. Tell the brethren to keep their hearts open to conviction, so that when the Holy Ghost comes to them, their hearts will be ready to receive it."[2]

Whenever I think about being prompted by the Holy Ghost, I recall the story of the two men on the road to Emmaus, discussing as they traveled how Jesus' body had been taken from the sepulcher. The Savior Himself drew near and talked with them, teaching them along the way, although in their grief they did not recognize Him. As He departed, they said one to another, "Did not our heart burn within us, while he talked with us by the way, and while he opened to us the scriptures?" (Luke 24: 31, 32).

As I look back on the "celestial heartburn" I have received along my journey to Bethlehem, I know that my heart truly has burned within me with a stronger testimony of the Savior and His example of endless love and compassion. I am so grateful for and have come to cherish the times when I feel this celestial heartburn within me because the still, quiet voice prompts me to action. I have the assurance that through the Holy Ghost, our Father will fill our lives with truth to the extent that we are willing to receive it. The only barriers to truth are the ones we place upon ourselves.

As we heed the promptings we receive, the Lord will allow us to be His hands to help those around us, and we might not even be aware of it at the time. I experienced an example of this during a recent Thanksgiving when the Lord blessed my family.

For years, I have wanted to forgo our traditional dinner in order to help serve a meal to the homeless, and we had made the decision to do so. However, as we were making arrangements, I kept getting a persistent feeling that it wasn't the right thing to do. Reluctantly, I decided to heed the prompting, and instead we held a traditional Thanksgiving dinner at our house for my husband's parents and other family members. We had a nice dinner and a great visit with the family. My mother-in-law, who had been struggling with Parkinson's disease, seemed particularly radiant and happy to be there. She had a chance to see many of her grandchildren, most of whom she hadn't seen in over a year, and she really seemed to enjoy herself. In fact, she looked better than I had seen her for a couple of years. After dinner, she thanked me through tears for all the effort I had gone through, and she seemed peaceful and content when it was time for them to leave.

While kneeling in prayer and contemplating the events at the end of the day, the thought came to me, "What if this is the last Thanksgiving we will ever be able to spend with my husband's parents?" Tears filled my eyes and gratitude filled my heart for the opportunity to have them there. Tired but happy, I climbed into bed with the thought that perhaps next year would finally bring the chance to serve at the homeless shelter.

Early the next morning, we received a telephone call informing us that my mother-in-law had passed away from a heart attack. I became suddenly aware of the precious gift the Lord had given us of one last opportunity to have her with us. She had been blessed to be able to see her family, and we had been blessed to have her there. But it was at the funeral, while conversing with many of her grandchildren, that I realized how important it had been for them to have that time to share with her.

I know that the Holy Ghost will teach us and lead us to the opportunities that can help us teach, enjoy, and inspire our family members, friends, neighbors, and strangers. If there is anything worthwhile that might come from the pages of this book, I pray that it will be a conviction to seek out the Spirit more fully each and every day. Follow your heart and the direction that it tells you to go. And if this direction is not in step with what the world is doing, then have the courage to step out of line. We can be like those wise men of old who "being warned of God in a dream that they should not return to Herod, they departed into their own country another way" (Matthew 2:12). We too can go home another way.

It is also my hope that I have motivated a closer evaluation of family traditions. It's not enough to do things just because that's the way we've always done them. We must think about our traditions and decide whether or not they bring us closer to our Savior and enrich our family bonds. The traditions that we choose should bring us together as forever families and strengthen our resolve to be together in Christ.

We need to remember that traditions are not the starting point of wonderful family celebrations but rather the consequences of such. By following the six steps that I have outlined, I know that Christmas can be grounded in our love for the Lord. Our purposes for celebrating will shine brightly like a candle that cannot be hidden. The intents of our hearts and our actions will be aligned together, and they will not be obscured by Satan's attempts to divert us from our chosen path.

As I have personally strived to pull away from the world and toward the Savior, I have been fortified by the responses of my family. My loving husband has been an example to me from the first Christmas that we spent together as newlyweds. We were going to school, and we had only a small amount of money that we could spend on each other. We decided to buy ourselves some ornaments to decorate our houseplant as our tree, and the rest we would spend on toys for a family that had come from Africa a few days before. They had two small children, and they had come with nothing but the clothes on their backs. With our meager amount of money, we were able to buy some presents that would be greatly appreciated. We placed the box of wrapped toys on the doorstep, rang the doorbell, and hurried away to our apartment, filled with the Spirit and comforted with a full portion of joy. We could not have asked for a better Christmas to begin our lives together.

Throughout the years, our efforts have not always been met with success, but ultimately our family has been blessed beyond my expectations. Confirmation of this came to me one evening in December when I noticed that my daughter Carianne, who had just turned ten, was deep in thought as she sat looking at the Christmas tree. I took the opportunity and asked her to describe to me what Christmas meant to her. Having a pen nearby, I quickly wrote down her reply word for word: "I think Christmas is sitting in your living room looking out into the snow, and the sky looks like a beautiful dark blue color over the shiny snow. Looking at the lights on the Christmas tree, feeling all peaceful inside and loving life, sitting there and thinking about Jesus and grateful about His gifts to us. The ground, covered with white, looks so pretty, and love is in the air so much it feels like you're wrapped up in it."

I was truly humbled by her reply, and it filled my heart to have this witness that our efforts had made a difference. She did not even mention Santa Claus, his gifts, or even waiting anxiously to open presents on Christmas Day. She talked only of peacefulness, of love, and of Jesus and His gifts to us. How grateful I was that I had struggled to make my way to Bethlehem.

What began as a journey of the wise men with their precious gifts to the Savior continues in our day as wise men and women still seek Him. Neal A. Maxwell said the following words of inspiration:

> Like the Wise Men from the east, we too must travel a great distance in order to come unto Christ, the Light of the World. No matter—He waits for us 'with open arms' (Mormon 6:17). May Christmas cause us deeper contemplation and deeper determination to complete that journey, the journey of journeys—in order to experience that resplendent rendezvous. . . .
>
> We can be like the Wise Men and notice the signs in the midst of an unnoticing world and seek the Savior—refusing, as did the Wise Men, to be used improperly by earthly rulers, yet giving freely of our gifts and talents and time, for these are the real gold, frankincense, and myrrh of our lives. . . .
>
> Like the Wise Men who persisted to Bethlehem, let us not turn back from our full journey—beyond Bethlehem—and we too shall be led to Him.[3]

Christmas should be the beginning of our journey beyond Bethlehem. A journey of love, of service, and of devotion as we follow His footsteps every day of the year. I know that the Savior Jesus Christ is the one perfect guide and that He came to earth to bless our lives and provide the light to illuminate our pathway back to Him. And like Moroni, I would also "commend you to seek this Jesus of whom the prophets and apostles have written, that the grace of God the Father, and also the Lord Jesus Christ, and the Holy Ghost, which beareth record of them, may be and abide in you forever. Amen" (Ether 12:41).

Notes
1. Neal A. Maxwell, *The Promise of Discipleship* (Salt Lake City: Deseret Book, 2001), 65.
2. Elden J. Watson, comp., *Manuscript History of Brigham Young 1846–1847*, (Salt Lake City: Elden J. Watson, 1971), as cited by Elder Neal A. Maxwell, *The Promise of Discipleship*, 104.
3. Elder Neal A. Maxwell, *The Christmas Scene* (Salt Lake City: Deseret Book, 1994) 12–14.

about the author

Denise Wamsley has always loved the true meaning of Christmas. Although shew grew up in a mixed-religion family, she found her heart longing to know more about Christ, and the celebration of His birth was a part of her conversion to Mormonism.

Because her father was in the U.S. Air Force, Denise lived in many locations during her youth but settled in Salt Lake City and graduated from Olympus High School. She attended Utah State University and Weber State University, and is a certified medical coder. She recently retired from the Utah College of Applied Technology, where she taught administrative medial assisting courses and was the Program Director for Medical Coding. Denise has taught not only as a profession but also as a way of sharing with others the passion she feels about Christmas.

She and her husband of thirty-plus years are the parents of four children and grandparents of eight. She currently lives in Smithfield, Utah, where she loves to celebrate Christmas in a way that she hopes honors the Savior whose name the holiday bears.

0 26575 59752 3